Building a good life for older people in local communities

Building a good life for older people in local communities

The experience of ageing in time and place

Mary Godfrey, Jean Townsend and Tracy Denby

JR
JOSEPH
ROWNTREE
FOUNDATION
1904
2004

The **Joseph Rowntree Foundation** has supported this project as part of its programme of research and innovative development projects, which it hopes will be of value to policy makers, practitioners and service users. The facts presented and views expressed in this report are, however, those of the authors and not necessarily those of the Foundation.

Joseph Rowntree Foundation
The Homestead
40 Water End
York
YO30 6WP
Website: www.jrf.org.uk

ISBN 1 85935 234 0 (paperback)
ISBN 1 85935 235 9 (pdf: available at www.jrf.org.uk)

A CIP catalogue record for this report is available from the British Library.

Cover design by Adkins Design

Prepared and printed by:
York Publishing Services Ltd
64 Hallfield Road
Layerthorpe
York
YO31 7ZQ
Tel: 01904 430033 Fax: 01904 430868 Website: www.yps-publishing.co.uk

Further copies of this report, or any other JRF publication, can be obtained either from the JRF website (www.jrf.org.uk/bookshop/) or from our distributor, York Publishing Services Ltd, at the above address.

CONTENTS

ACKNOWLEDGEMENTS

This study would not have been possible without the active support, enthusiasm and participation of older people. They gave generously of their time and contributed in many different ways: letting us see a glimpse of their lives, sharing with us their experiences and views, and allowing us to participate in some of their group activities.

We owe particular gratitude to the two groups in Leeds and Hartlepool: Caring Together and the Retired Resource Network, respectively. The Caring Together management committee and staff smoothed our path and generated interest in the study among members. RRN members welcomed us into their group meetings and gave up precious time to talk to us at length about what quality of life meant to them.

There are a number of individuals who participated as co-researchers in the study, and whose contribution we wish to acknowledge: Cherril Cliff, Sue Egan, Marion Dexter, Betty Lowe, Joan Simpson and Beatrice Stead. Their participation in different facets of the research – whether collecting the information, reflecting on its meaning or contributing to the report – not only challenged our thinking about ageing but demonstrated the mutual benefits of breaking down the traditional boundary between 'researcher' and 'researched'. It was a privilege to work with them and learn from them.

We must also thank the Joseph Rowntree Foundation who funded the research and the members of our Advisory Group who provided support and assistance throughout: Alex O'Neill from the Foundation, Stan Davison of the London Pensioners Forum, Professor Jill Manthorpe, formerly at Hull University and now at King's College London, and Charles Patmore from the Social Policy Research Unit at York University. From the very outset, Alex, in his role of steering through the project, established an enabling and trusting environment that allowed us to raise difficult problems in the expectation that solutions – albeit often messy – could be found.

Colleagues at the Nuffield Institute, Brian Hardy and Gill Callaghan, offered very helpful comments on earlier drafts; and our secretaries, Maureen Hutchinson and David Brennan, worked hard in producing, checking and making sense of our many drafts.

In a study such as this, it is perhaps inevitable that some of the people whom we interviewed and whom we got to know well died in the course of the research. Our commitment to confidentiality means we cannot name them or even refer to the pseudonyms we have used for them in the report. Their experiences and voices are reflected, however. We acknowledge their contribution and offer our sympathy to their friends and relatives.

1 BACKGROUND AND CONTEXT

Introduction

This report is about the experience of ageing in two localities. Older people, from across the age spectrum, talk to us about their lives and about their friends, family and the neighbourhoods in which they live. They describe the opportunities and challenges of getting old and shed light on what makes for a 'good life' in old age. Their experiences and views offer insight into the kinds of services and support that might sustain well-being as people get older.

Quality of life in ageing

At a general level, research has identified a number of broad aspirations common to people in later life: independence and autonomy, being active and included, having choices and being in control of one's life. These themes are reflected and reinforced within the current government's policy priorities. The modernisation agenda for health and social care services places emphasis on reducing dependence through prevention and rehabilitation. The thrust of regeneration and renewal strategies, involving local communities, is to reduce social and economic inequalities, secure health and well-being at an individual and collective level and facilitate social inclusion. The values and goals underpinning the Better Government for Older People programme initiated by the Cabinet Office emphasise working with older people, to promote independence, choice and integration.

Our concern in this study, however, was to delve beneath the general aspirations associated with quality of life and to explore how older people construct a good life. But whilst we take ageing as our starting point, we also recognise that there is considerable diversity among people who are older. On the one hand, socio-economic position, gender and ethnicity influence attitudes to, and the experience of, ageing. On the other hand, given the span of years covered by the term 'old age', it is likely to encompass very varied circumstances and experiences. Underpinning our interest in quality of life, then, were the following questions. How does the meaning and experience of ageing reflect people's life chances – the times through which they have lived, and the social, material and physical environments that comprise the backdrop to, and structure the rhythm of, daily living? Are the factors that make for a good life the same for 'younger' old people, as well as those in advanced old age? Does the meaning of such values as independence and inclusion remain the same across the process of ageing? How can an understanding of this diversity in old age facilitate a more accurate, user-centred approach to service planning and development to support well-being?

The duality of ageing

Ageing and old age have been subjected to negative and positive stereotyping. The first – or 'deficit' model – views old age as an unremitting period of loss, decline and social withdrawal. The second – or 'heroic' model – considers 'active' or 'successful' ageing in terms of being fit, healthy and happy. Both are problematic. The deficit model not only denies the accomplishments of ageing, but reinforces the devaluing of older people and the view of them as passive recipients of services. The heroic model implies that to experience loss – of health or abilities – is to age 'badly', what

Andrews (1999) terms 'the seductiveness of agelessness'. Within this schema, according to Andrews, to age well means 'not to age at all, or at least to minimise the extent to which it is apparent that one is ageing, both internally and externally' (1999, p. 305). Such a conception, she argues, is to deny the experience of years – how people have developed in response to the challenges of everyday life, challenges that in later years also contain within them the possibility of the emergence of capacities that may improve with age. For Andrews the key problem is how to locate and represent both continuity and transformation in old age, i.e. a continuation of the self and the life that has been lived and the changes that occur physically, socially and psychologically over the ageing process.

In exploring well-being in old age, our underpinning rationale is the duality of ageing – the tension between old age as being both about loss and adjustment, and opportunities for personal development and growth. Moreover, older people are seeking to make sense of, and are actively engaged in, a process of adaptation to physical, social, interpersonal and psychological changes, embracing both learning and adjustment. Within the field of life-span developmental psychology, Paul Baltes and colleagues (Baltes and Baltes, 1990; Baltes and Carstensen, 1996) have specified three processes whereby the person manages these changes: namely, selection, compensation and optimisation. At a very simple level, for example, the passionate gardener may maintain interest into old age by reducing the size of the borders and concentrating on low-maintenance shrubs (*selection*), constructing raised beds for ease of access (*compensation*) and placing the emphasis on creating painterly schemes within a small space (*optimisation*). They also suggest, however, that the balance of losses over gains may become more pronounced with advancing age.

This model focuses attention on the lived experience of ageing and frames the questions of interest in terms that do not deny its reality. For example:

- How do people make sense of ageing and what are the things that matter to them to maintain well-being?

- How do they make the most of opportunities and manage or adjust to the changes that accompany ageing?

- Are there particular kinds of transitions or changes that occur in older age which offer opportunities for growth and 'flowering'?

- Are there, conversely, transitions or changes that threaten or disrupt well-being and erode a positive image of self?

- How can an understanding of the process of adaptation enable us to construct service responses that compensate for loss and optimise opportunities?

As we indicated above, whilst there are facets of ageing that are common to us all, there are also important differences between older people in how they experience ageing that reflect the wider socio-economic context of their lives. Thus, there is considerable evidence that material factors – income, occupation, social class – affect health and functional ability in old age. Similarly, people vary in the resources available to them in forging adaptive responses to life changes – whether at the psychological, interpersonal, community or societal level. Moreover, the meaning and experience of ageing and the values that underpin what is conceived of as a 'good life' will vary over time and across cultures. Riley (1998) uses the metaphor of the escalator for ageing, suggesting that, as people age, they move diagonally upward and across time. But unlike the static floor over which the escalator is moving, the social structures surrounding people's lives – at work, at home, in the community – are continually changing. A major challenge, therefore, in understanding ageing is how to examine the relationship between individual lives and the wider social structures which both shape those lives and are in turn influenced by the action of individuals. In developing the framework for the study, then, our starting point was a model of ageing which locates individual experience within a broader socio-economic and cultural context (Godfrey, 2001) and is set out in Figure 1 below.

Figure 1 Social–cultural model of successful ageing

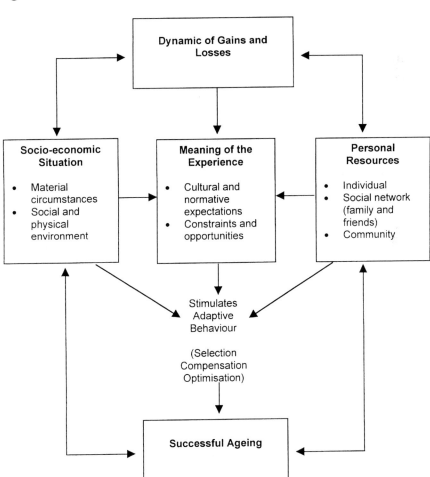

Ageing in place

In this study, interest in exploring the social and cultural context of well-being in old age led us to focus on ageing in different places. We considered that this would allow us, first, to connect the experiences of older people's daily lives with the characteristics of the settings in which they lived. Second, it would enable us to work with groups of older people to identify the kinds of services/opportunities that would support a good life in old age. Third, it would help to frame solutions in the context of the kinds of places and people that form the canvas on which the experience of ageing is painted. Key questions posed here, then, were:

- How important to older people were the localities in which they lived? In what ways did they shape the experience of ageing?

- What were the features of localities that sustained people in old age or alternatively were seen as a threat to well-being?

- In what ways did people's location within a specific historical and cultural context shape their current beliefs and values about 'healthy ageing'?

- What were the salient events and experiences in their lives that were viewed as significant for their self-identity and well-being in old age?

- What kinds of resources were available to older people within particular localities that they could draw upon in optimising opportunities and developing adaptive responses to ageing?

- What could we learn about service models and approaches that would be effective to support 'successful' ageing?

The localities we chose to study were selected for a number of reasons. From a practical point of view, the fact that we had some prior knowledge of the areas and of older people's groups within them meant that we had some common ground from which to present the idea of a partnership in the development of the project. As both are located in the North of England, within relatively easy access for the researchers, we could spend time within the localities to develop a more in-depth picture of life (although this proved not so clear-cut, as we discuss in Chapter 2).

Both localities, albeit in different ways, reflect a microcosm of some of the kinds of socio-economic changes that have enveloped towns and cities in England over several decades. One of them – Woodhouse and Little London – is an inner-city area of Leeds, a fast-growing, affluent city, home to many of the regional headquarters of large companies, finance and banking establishments. In the past a traditional working-class neighbourhood, it now displays many features of urban deprivation as the factories and industries on which people depended for work have long since disappeared. The other locality – Hartlepool – is a North East town that has experienced major deindustrialisation and unemployment within the working lives of those who are now in their seventies and eighties. This decline has also marked the lives of their adult children in myriad ways.

Developing a partnership with older people

A distinctive feature of the research was the adoption of a participatory approach to the study, seeking to involve established groups of older people in partnership with researchers, developing the design, collecting the information and contributing to the analysis and write-up of the report. The thinking underpinning this approach was twofold. First, it was hoped that such a process would build capacity within the groups that would be a resource in developing future activities. Second, it was felt that the active participation of older people would enrich the research: by drawing on their knowledge of the locality, including existing social networks to identify older people of varied circumstances, experiences and relationships to formal services; and by combining their expertise and understanding of both the ageing process and campaigning activity with the formal knowledge and training of the research team.

Two established networks of older people were invited to participate. The Caring Together group operates within the Woodhouse/Little London area of Leeds, with a population of about 8,200 people, 18 per cent of whom are over 60 years of age (somewhat lower than the city as a whole at 21 per cent). The area has a significant minority ethnic population (17 per cent compared to 6 per cent for Leeds) – mainly of African-Caribbean origin but of South Asian origin as well. This has a younger profile than the white population, with only 4 per cent over the age of 60 years. The Retired Resource Network operates across the town of Hartlepool, with a primarily white (99 per cent) population of around 89,000 people. The character of the two groups is very different as the pen-pictures in Box 1 and Box 2 in the following pages reveal.

Summary

The study sought to explore with older people themselves the meaning of well-being over the ageing process. By developing understanding of what was meant by a 'good' old age, we hoped to gain insight into what kinds of services/support would sustain well-being as people got older.

The research was carried out within two urban areas: an inner-city locality and a northern town. The locality focus, we considered, would allow us to examine ageing in context. In particular, we were interested in looking at how the wider structures within which older people lived their lives affected both their adaptive responses to ageing and the resources available to them to manage the process.

An important facet of the research was the adoption of a participatory approach to the study. We sought to involve older people in every aspect of the research – developing the ideas, collecting the information, contributing to the writing and drawing out the conclusions. Our objectives here were twofold: to enrich the research through mutual learning between researchers and older people; and to help build capacity within the groups, as a resource for the future.

Box 1 Profile of Caring Together

Caring Together, a registered charity, was established formally in 1994, in Woodhouse and Little London, an ethnically diverse inner-city area of Leeds. It is one of 37 neighbourhood network schemes around Leeds that support and engage older people within local communities. Many of these, like Caring Together, had their origins in local community groups that were developed and extended as part of the community care strategy of the social services department in the early

Caring Together's Research Advisory Group

(Continued overleaf)

1990s. The schemes are independent charities, drawing on a range of funding sources, including the local authority, and are managed by local people who decide what they want from their scheme.

Caring Together provides advice, advocacy and support to older people (housing, social services and welfare rights), organises social and leisure activities (gentle exercise and keep-fit groups, art and crafts, theatre trips, outings, coffee mornings, friendship groups), facilitates mutual support and exchange through befriending and volunteering and provides a gardening and decorating service.

Older people play a leading role in planning, developing and participating in the work of the group at all levels – organising social and educational activities, acting as befrienders and being members of the management committee. Membership is open to those over 60 years in the locality. With some 370 members, this is approximately one quarter of older people in the area. It is supported by a small staff team (project co-ordinator, community volunteer co-ordinator, neighbourhood development worker, activities organiser and part-time administrator).

The group receives a small amount of funding from Leeds Social Services Department (approximately £20,000 a year). The balance of some £80,000 for staffing and activities is raised through time-limited funding from such sources as the National Lottery Charities Board, Comic Relief and the Esme Fairburn Foundation.

Box 2 Profile of the Retired Resource Network (RRN)

The RRN was set up in November 1997 in Hartlepool, prompted by Anchor Trust's local service network initiative. Its aim was to bring together retired people in the town to offer mutual support, develop confidence and skills and campaign around issues of relevance to older people. In 1999, it became one of 28 pilot schemes under the Better Government for Older People programme and was constituted

Members of the RRN

as a charity. In 2000, it was one of the projects supported by the community development team in Hartlepool. This team, managed by Anchor Trust, was funded through a partnership grant from Hartlepool Social Services Department.

From small beginnings, the RRN quickly developed as a town-wide group, comprised of, and run by, retired people. In its first two to three years it involved some 50 older people, meeting fortnightly in the community centre in Owton Manor – located in the south west of the town, an area of high unemployment (21 per cent), and dominated by social rented housing (65 per cent). It organised a number of successful campaigns to improve services (bus shelter, seating in the shopping centre), facilitated access to courses (using computers, art, first aid) and ran a well-attended event on housing options for older people. It also spawned a friendship group, meeting weekly, that offered a forum for older people to meet together for companionship and sociability. Group members also participated in local planning forums with health and social services agencies.

2 APPROACH AND PARTNERSHIP

The research approach

Drawing on the lived experiences of older people in two localities, the aims of the study were to:

- examine what was important to people to maintain quality of life over the ageing process

- work alongside older people to develop understanding of service preferences and priorities that would sustain a 'good life' in old age

- create a partnership with a group of older people within each of two localities to develop and carry out the research.

The research began in May 2001. In the discussion below, we describe, first, how we went about developing understanding of well-being in ageing. Second, we consider the approach adopted in translating these quality of life themes into service preferences and priorities to sustain 'successful' ageing. Third, we examine the development of the partnership with the older people's groups and the factors that both inhibited and facilitated joint working.

Exploring quality of life

In exploring well-being, we used a range of information collection methods:

- in-depth, one-to-one interviews with older people, using a biographical or life story approach

- focus group interviews examining key transitions over the ageing process (e.g. retirement), strategies for keeping well and managing loss (e.g. maintaining health and well-being, coping with bereavement and ill health) and service priorities to sustain life quality in old age

- participant observation in the older people's groups (attending group meetings and activities, informal discussions with participants about life in the area and what was important for them)

- building up a picture of local networks within which older people were embedded through interviewing key informants active in the community (from tenants associations, churches and community groups, day centres and sheltered housing schemes, and older people's organisations (e.g. Age Concern, Older People's Forum).

Life story interview

The life story interview is a particular form of the in-depth interview, described as a 'conversation with a purpose' (Burgess, 1984, p. 102). As with the in-depth interview, its objective is to see the world from the perspective of the person being interviewed; to explore *why* people act as they do and the meaning they attach to their actions. Additionally, the life story approach seeks to understand how the person develops over time and to locate individual experiences and meanings within a cultural and historical context. In our study, using this method enabled us to explore the meaning of ageing dynamically as the consequence of past experience and circumstances, current situation and future expectations. This occurred in two ways. First, by locating older people's lives in time and place, we were able to examine how both the general and unique aspects of the individual's life story affected their views of well-being as they got older. In what ways, for example, had major social events like the Second World War impacted on the individual's life course and shaped perceptions and expectations of life in old age? How had the experience of caring for parents and other relatives informed older people's perceptions of what was right and proper to demand of their families as they got older? Second, it facilitated understanding of the interplay between individuals' goals and aspirations and the kinds of constraints operating on people over the life course. Thus, we could see how the cultural, social, material and economic circumstances of people's lives had affected both their life chances and health in old age and the resources available to them to adapt to the changes wrought by the ageing process.

The following broad themes or topics provided the structure within which people told their stories:

- growing up and growing old in particular places

- life stages, formative influences and relationships over time and place (schooling, work, significant events, family, friends, neighbours)

- transitions and changes over the ageing process – the meaning of these for the individual and how they have managed them.

A significant aspect of the life story approach with older people was the way in which telling their story validated and affirmed the value and importance of people's individual lives. It facilitated the process of remembering and expressing the strengths, insights and difficulties overcome as well as the constraints on opportunities experienced over a lifetime.

Sampling strategy

People were purposively selected to ensure inclusion of older people across the age spectrum, in different circumstances (living alone/with a partner; men/women), with different experiences of loss (e.g. widowed, varied levels of disability) and from different minority ethnic groups (Leeds only: African-Caribbean and Asian). The Appendix describes the sample in more detail. People were accessed through a variety of routes. Within Leeds, people were initially contacted through Caring Together staff and members although their relationship to the group varied considerably, from those who were active participants in activities to members who were receiving considerable support from the group in their own homes. We also sought to include older people in the local community who were not involved with the group, using a range of methods – via friends and acquaintances of older people interviewed, and via other community organisations (community centre and churches) and sheltered housing schemes. A small number of people were contacted through the social services department, selected on the basis that they were high users of home care services (at least once a day), to explore similarities and differences with those whose main source of support was

Caring Together. Within Hartlepool, most of those involved in the RRN during the period of study were interviewed formally on two occasions (in addition to informal discussion, during and following meetings). A small number of more disabled older people were recruited through the social services department (via a day centre) and through direct contact with wardens in a number of local sheltered housing schemes.

A total of 84 individuals were interviewed using the life story method – 62 in Leeds (within 54 interviews some of which were couples together) and 22 in Hartlepool (within 29 separate interviews, including some couples together and 11 interviewed on two separate occasions). The average length of interview was 90 minutes. Caring Together staff and older people carried out half of the one-to-one interviews in Leeds and were trained and supported by the Nuffield researchers. The Nuffield researchers did all of the interviews in Hartlepool.

Focus groups

As an adjunct to the biographical interviews, we organised focus groups with older people in a range of settings, to deepen understanding of key points of transition and the strategies people engaged in to adapt to the changes in their lives. Most were either established groups or involved people who were known to each other. It was notable that in describing facets of their life and what it meant to grow old, people within the groups recounted stories about people, places and events that generated and affirmed shared memories and values. These in turn reinforced both their sense of identity and the way in which their individual lives were linked with others with similar experiences.

Five focus groups were organised within Leeds: two sessions with seven older people who played a leading role in Caring Together; one group of five people who had limited mobility; a small group (four) attending the local day centre and another group of community activists (three people). In Hartlepool, there were five groups comprising RRN members, four of which occurred within the framework of the regular fortnightly meetings of the group (15, 13, 17 and 16 people) and one that was held separately (six people). A further group of older people attending a local day centre (five people) was also organised.

Understanding service preferences and priorities

Following the interviews on the quality of life theme, researchers carried out an initial analysis of the material to draw out the implications for service planning and development. These were discussed and reflected upon within a number of workshops organised with older people and staff from Caring Together and in a joint one-day event that brought together members of Caring Together and the RRN. The discussions framed the initial topic guide for a series of focus groups held during November and December 2002, in Leeds and Hartlepool. A total of 58 older people participated in six focus groups. Three of these were held in Woodhouse, two in Little London, and one in Hartlepool. An interview with a representative of a city-wide Leeds group was also undertaken. One group was with active older people who were involved in community representation, two were with older people who were able to get out and about and three involved people who were restricted as a result of health and mobility problems. The last five were established social groups of older people, who were not accustomed to discussing service priorities.

The first focus group comprised ten older people with limited mobility. They were enabled to attend by the provision of door-to-door transport. Findings from the research were introduced and people's ideas about how services could be provided to enhance older people's quality of life were invited. The initial reaction was to express satisfaction with existing services and to react defensively:

> I think they are all doing their best. You can't improve on what they are doing.

Taking the wider aspects of physical and social environment such as safety and transport as a starting point, a number of service priorities were raised: on balance, the discussion remained rooted in people's own direct experience of existing services and they struggled with the breadth of the task of discussing service developments and improvements.

We decided, therefore, to adopt an alternative approach at the following focus group, and to use vignettes describing the circumstances of two imaginary older people, living in the neighbourhood. The use of vignettes appeared to create a distance between those 'in need' and group members. One of the characters, 'Ada', was restricted to her house by severe mobility problems; although her family continued to be important, her network of friends was contracting. The second character, 'Joe', lived alone in a high-rise flat, without any close family or friends but with a neighbour who kept an eye on him. He could get out each day to the shops and the local pub. He was becoming slightly confused, his house was described as 'a bit of a mess' and he had been prey to con men.

The second focus group – of women in their sixties and seventies, who were restricted to their homes because of ill health – found common cause with Ada's experience. The discussion flowed easily and the values attached to independence and managing one's own life that had been explicit in the quality of life interviews were asserted. The importance of social contact was highlighted. The discussion of Joe's needs was also rooted in their personal experiences with male relatives. As the focus groups progressed we continued to use a combination of the vignettes and the dimensions-of-need framework.

Several observations about the nature of the evidence from the focus groups are important to note. When asked to reflect on features of life quality for older people restricted by ill health or immobility, group participants drew almost exclusively on their own personal experiences, either direct or indirect. Some of the younger, more active group members showed less understanding of what might inhibit social engagement for frailer people. One consequence was that those who drew upon their own experience of restrictions retained a more person-centred approach when thinking about support options. Some of the active elders, however, were more distanced and focused on formal service provision. Some discussions, for example, began with an assumption that if an older person had an assessment or attended a day centre, their needs would be met.

There was a particular issue relating to older people with dementia. In the general group discussions, there was a sense of 'otherness' and distance from people with dementia, which generated views that 'these people' should be 'looked after'. This contrasted with evidence, presented elsewhere in the report, of individual caring responsibilities borne by spouses, siblings and friends for older people who were confused.

Concepts of choice and control which were so significant when people talked about what was important for their own quality of life assumed less prominence when service provision was being discussed. It seemed that because we had framed the discussion around services rather than life quality, people's ideas were more bounded by the perceived realities of known service provision. Thus, people tended to talk about what was available, rather than describe their visions of a different future.

Key issues arose around consideration of services for older people who were not well represented in the groups. For example, because the majority of those participating were women, there was recognition that men might have different needs and priorities but there was less clarity about how these might be addressed.

Within the complexities outlined above, a rich vein of data was drawn from the focus groups, both confirming the experiences of services described by individual older people in their one-to-one interviews and identifying and elaborating on unmet needs and service preferences. However, they also laid bare the importance of clarity about whose voices are being heard when involving people in service development and planning.

Partnership working

With each of the older people's groups – Caring Together and the RRN – we adopted a similar approach towards developing mutual understanding, trust and engagement in the project. We participated in meetings, talked to people individually and attended different group events. We also organised two exchange visits for RRN and Caring Together members in Leeds and Hartlepool for people to share experiences, consider differences and similarities in problems they encountered and gain insight into the different ways of organising in their respective localities. Even so, the nature of the partnerships that evolved was very different across the two sites. We examine what was achieved and the factors that contributed to the varied experience of partnership working.

Caring Together

Within Leeds, with the support of the management committee, a steering group was established, initially comprised of four older people active in Caring Together and chaired by the group's co-ordinator. This met on a regular basis (six-weekly) throughout the project to plan and review the work. Membership was open in that those who expressed an interest at any point were drawn in, expanding its size over the life of the study.

Over a two-year period, the partnership facilitated the development of mutually reinforcing skills and expertise. Researchers trained and supported a small number of older people to carry out qualitative interviews with others in their own locality, using existing networks and contacts to embrace people of varied circumstances – from those active in the community to those who were frail and relatively isolated. A process of support and feedback was put in place for the 'trainee researchers', to develop their confidence and skills and to enable the 'professional researchers' to draw on the insights that the older people brought to the project. This helped to maintain the involvement of the interviewers and reinforced for everyone that training was a continual learning process for all members of the team.

The forging of the partnership was gradual and incremental with each aspect of the activity feeding into and expanding enthusiasm and confidence to take on new tasks. Thus, involving older people in the interviewing was extended to encompass analysis and writing up the research. We experimented with different approaches to engaging people effectively (for example, through iterative reflections on their own experience and the emerging data, workshops to explore how themes and relationships across a number of interviews could be built up, and incorporating taped discussions with group members into the writing).

Involving older people in qualitative researching within their own neighbourhoods raised important issues for the research team. Whilst it was invaluable in enabling us to build up a rich seam of local knowledge of value to the project, we had to carefully work through with older people the likely impact of the research on their social relationships within the locality. How would they be viewed by people who were acquainted with them in different contexts? Would they be seen as 'busybodies'? How could they suspend their own commonly held assumptions to probe people's exact meanings in the interview situation? For staff too, could they move out of 'helping' or 'assessing' mode to engage people in 'conversation' about their lives? Support that involved researchers in listening to the taped interviews, feeding back comments to the interviewer and both reflecting on what was produced proved an essential part of skills development – for both sets of partners. The value of the approach was that the content of their interviews revealed a degree of empathy and mutual understanding such that older people were more able to present both the positives and negatives of ageing. They did not appear to have the same difficulties in getting beyond the 'heroic' presentation of ageing that the other members of the research team experienced.

Active participation of staff and members in formal and informal discussion and feedback with individuals through the steering group, the management committee, review workshops and the annual general meetings were seen as invaluable in enabling the group to reflect on what it did well and what it could do better. The research reinforced and brought to the foreground the strength and value of the community development model that so resonated with older people; the importance they attached to solidarity and reciprocal exchanges, built upon and sustained through the varied activities and ways of working of Caring Together; and the opportunities afforded to 'give something to the community', to make a better life for themselves and others.

For those individual older people who participated as researchers and in the steering group, involvement was seen as enjoyable and worthwhile and also developed skills and confidence. At the same time, feedback on the writing illustrated the importance attached to 'giving voice': seeing their words on paper not only gave value to their unique, personal experience but it also underscored what was common and shared with others in similar circumstances – thereby locating the individual within a wider social context.

Retired Resource Network

With the RRN, individuals were extremely hospitable, open and generous with their time and welcomed us in the group. We were, however, only able to move beyond the traditional researcher/researched relationship to a very limited extent during the life of the project. Thus, while members were keen to explore with us what quality of life and well-being meant to them, both within the group and individually, we did not succeed in engaging them in 'researching' older people beyond the group. Neither were we able to access other older people through the RRN. Members of the group, moreover, were disappointed at the outcome: they considered they had learned little from the study.

Learning the lessons

It is evident that there are many layers of explanatory factors that account for the very different experience of partnership working across the two localities. Some reflect the individual personalities involved and the degree of trust and empathy that the researchers were able to develop within the two groups. Others relate to the nature of the groups, the contexts in which they operated, their size and stage of development, and the perceived usefulness of the research in developing their vision for the future. Since these latter are of wider import to partnership working, we examine them below.

Group context

Caring Together has a large membership base (around 370 people) and operates within a well-defined geographical area from which its members are drawn. It has a rich group life, involving a wide range of older people in different relationships to the group. There is a weekly cycle of social, leisure and activity groups (gentle exercise, art and crafts, friendship); regular, albeit less frequent planning groups (e.g. volunteers, fundraising and social events, management committee); and broad-based one-off events that involve a considerably larger group of older people living in the locality (e.g. summer fair, fashion show, sponsored walk, Christmas party, day trips and visits to the theatre). At its core is a nucleus of five paid staff (three of whom are full-time and two part-time). These have an in-depth knowledge of the local area and a commitment to, and interest in, exploring new and creative ways of responding to the diverse needs of older people within the locality, drawing out and building on their skills and expertise and offering a range of opportunities for engaging them in the life of the group. The early familiarisation process therefore involved the 'professional' researcher in formal and informal meetings in many different settings with large numbers of older people to introduce the project and to develop a picture of community networks and the place of older people within them. We were therefore able not only to move within Caring Together but outwards from it, interviewing key informants within the locality, many of them older people with a rich history of campaigning and engagement in community development, for example within tenants groups, the community centre and local churches.

From the outset, the management committee was an active sponsor of the research. Committee and staff spent considerable time and effort seeking to smooth our path into the locality and generating enthusiasm for the project. Even so, initial steps on both sides were tentative and hesitant. Staff members were concerned about the potential for the research to raise expectations of them that they could not meet. Older people expressed a lack of familiarity with, and confidence in, their ability to actively contribute to the research. For everyone, there was uncertainty over the precise way in which the research could be integrated into and contribute to the development of the group, despite a general sense that this was possible. We were also very naive in the approach adopted at the beginning, expecting that group members would be able to shape the direction of the project. An important lesson in the early months of the study was the understanding that in order to form and develop a new partnership, it was not helpful to present an open agenda. It was only in the context of our setting clear objectives and negotiating steps towards their achievement that older people felt able to engage in a discussion about how they could make a contribution. A key step forward was taken with the setting up of two focus group interviews with leading activists. Although an aspect of the information gathering, these allowed members to experience qualitative research at first hand. As well as being extremely enjoyable for people, they could begin to see both how the information generated could be useful in arriving at a better understanding of older people in the area and how the group could reach out to those not involved. As people became more confident of how the research could contribute to their aspirations for the group, they assumed an increasingly active role in shaping the process.

The RRN is a relatively small group (around 20 members) comprised of older people – all of whom are working in a voluntary capacity. Unlike Caring Together, it has no paid workers to support the activity, although it did have some assistance from a community development worker early on (being a conduit for information about activities in the town relevant to older people, helping the group with applications for funding and providing some administrative assistance). The role of this worker was in the process of redefinition during the course of the study: as a consequence, the assistance was gradually withdrawn and by the end of the study the group was left on its own.

The RRN sees itself as a campaigning group to make life better for older people in the town of Hartlepool. Its membership, however, is drawn mainly from its southern end. The group meets fortnightly in a community centre on the boundary of the Owton Manor estate, which has a reputation as a 'sink' estate. The ward within which the centre is located is one of the most deprived not only in Hartlepool but nationally (ranked 25 of 8,414 in level of deprivation in England). At the time of the research, none of the members came from the estate; most lived in semi-detached, owner-occupied properties on its fringes or in adjacent wards of former council estates that are now in predominantly private ownership. There was no specific focus either on campaigning activity within the locality that might have drawn in older people from the area.

Individual members were also involved in other groups apart from the RRN. These included community organisations or social clubs centred on their immediate locality, town-based interest groups such as the Rotary Club or social and mutual support organisations like the Widows Association and Friendship Group. There was little or no overlap between membership in these varied groups and RRN members viewed their involvement in these different arenas as separate and distinct from their participation in the RRN. It had not always been like this. During the early days of the RRN the membership had come from a wider catchment area and people from some of these other groups were drawn into its campaigning activity. The Friendship Group, for example, had developed in parallel with the RRN, with a considerable overlap in membership in the early years but, with one exception, these had since dropped away from the RRN.

There were several facets of the organisation of the RRN, then, which combined together posed difficulties in working in a participatory way with the group. First, it was small in size and was reliant on the voluntary efforts of members. Second, group life was primarily bounded within the framework of the two-hour, fortnightly meetings. There were therefore few opportunities for the researchers to take part in arenas that extended beyond attendance at these meetings. Third, the group was not rooted in the local area and its activity during the period of the research did not engage older people within the locality. The RRN was therefore unable to provide an entrée to other older people in the area, and we were unable to convince members that involvement in the research might offer a focus for expanding the group. Thus, when we did access older people beyond the group through day centres and sheltered housing, RRN members felt unable to be involved in the information collection. In part this reflected the fact that they felt they had enough to do and did not wish to take on the additional work that participation in the research process would involve; in part it reflected difficulties in the group, considered below.

Size and stage of development of the groups

As indicated above, Caring Together is a well-established group with a large, diverse and expanding membership. Although it is confronted each year with the problem of securing sufficient funding to maintain its activities, it has been successful to the extent of not only sustaining its work but in expanding its range of activities. It is a group, moreover, that is engaged in ongoing reflection of the needs of older people in the locality and reviewing how it can develop flexible and creative ways of dealing with them.

The RRN was extremely successful in its first couple of years and at its highest point had a membership of some 50 people. As indicated in Chapter 1, it was also one of 28 pilot projects supported under the auspices of the Better Government for Older People initiative. At the start of the project in early summer of 2001, membership had more than halved and attendance at group meetings averaged 16 people. By the second year, attendance declined further to an average of 13 people. A consistent theme across interviews with individuals in the group was the loss of members over a sustained period and the difficulties experienced in involving new people in the group. Similarly, a major preoccupation within the meetings during the entire period of the study was the need to expand its membership base. Whilst those remaining held strongly to the view that its aims were worthwhile, their persistence owed much to their remembrance of past success and to their commitment as individuals to making things better for older people. It was notable that of those involved in the group during the study period, the majority had joined around the time of its formation or shortly after. A small number of people were recruited during the study but most of them did not stay for very long.

The declining size of the group had important implications for what it could hope to achieve. First, of those people who remained involved, many of them described very active lives: social, leisure and caring responsibilities, as well as participation in other social and community organisations. Others had, over the life of the group, become more frail and/or experienced ill health that limited their capacity for active involvement. In the one-to-one interviews as well, people expressed the view that whilst the group was important to them, they did not want to spend all of their time engaged in campaigning. Indeed, one aspect of the positive side of ageing from their perspective was that they could choose to do lots of different things they enjoyed doing and were not constrained by the kind of family and work responsibilities that they had carried during earlier stages of their lives. It was notable that older activists in Caring Together expressed similar sentiments. Whereas in the past they had taken on leading roles within community organisations, they relished the kind of involvement opportunities within Caring Together: active engagement without the full weight of day-to-day responsibilities being placed upon them. The dilemma for the RRN, however, was that membership was unlikely to expand without an active campaigning focus that would engage wider numbers of older people; yet their reduced numbers made this difficult to achieve.

Alongside the decline in membership of the RRN, and perhaps a factor in it, was its changed role within the town. As Better Government for Older People (BGOP) became established with a regional structure and regional representation, the RRN lost influence as other groups were established. A town-wide forum – the 50+ Group – was set up through the efforts of the community development team. In the form of an open meeting to which anyone over 50 years could attend, along with people from older people's groups in the town, this was the forum through which local health and social care agencies consulted on policy and service development, for example, the National Service Framework for Older People. It also sent representatives to the regional BGOP committee. Although RRN members took part in the forum, the group was just one of several others and had lost its pre-eminent position as a pilot BGOP site. These changes within the external environment also contributed to uncertainty about the group's purpose and direction.

Finally, the pattern and rhythm of the research project had peaks of hands-on activity for the groups (participating in focus groups and interviewing) but troughs when they felt more distanced from the process, particularly in the protracted phase of report writing. Within Leeds, involvement of members in the process of analysis and in the shaping of the report led to shared understanding of these facets of the research process. There was also a desire to move ahead to develop an action plan from the report and bring the research findings to a wider audience within the city. Within Hartlepool, given the more distant relationship between the group and the researchers, there was considerable frustration at the time involved between data collection and the written product.

Summary

The study adopted different methods to collect information: in-depth biographical interviews; focus groups; and participation in group events and activities. Selection of people to interview was done purposively – to ensure inclusion of older people across the age spectrum with varied circumstances and experiences.

The depth of partnership secured varied significantly between the two groups. Whereas Caring Together participated in all facets of the research and felt 'ownership' of the findings, we were unable to involve the RRN much beyond the traditional researcher/researched relationship. Certainly, size and stage of development of the respective groups were important explanatory factors in the level of participation achieved. The larger membership and richer group life of Caring Together presented more opportunities to engage people in the project flexibly, at different levels and with varying degrees of involvement. But fundamental to the success of the partnership here was the fact that members were able to see how the project could contribute to the work of the group. Whilst RRN members had an interest in the topic of the research, we were unable to convince the group that the study had relevance to its purpose and aims.

From our different experience with each of the groups, the following elements would appear to be critical in the development of effective research partnerships with older people:

- clarity on the part of the researchers about aims and objectives and use of different forums and media to communicate these directly to group members and to key decision makers

- the existence of a 'fit' between the group's objectives and those of the research and the perceived salience of the research given the group's stage of development

- time and opportunity to build up familiarity and trust with people

- willingness to try out different approaches that mesh with the organisational structures and capacity of the group

- the presence of research champions – 'insiders' or informants – that are trusted and respected by group members, as well as consistent ongoing support from the research team

- the opportunity to restate and reaffirm the aims and purpose of the work in different settings until people feel confident that they have understood them

- reassurance for people who are engaging in an unfamiliar task and the need to relate research methodology to their own experience

- availability of time, energy, interest and enthusiasm to become involved.

The absence of any of these elements is likely to impede an effective partnership. At the same time, it is not possible to anticipate all of them in advance and some will only be revealed in the course of constructing the partnership. Whilst the risks are considerable, the mutual strengths, rewards and achievements that success offers make the efforts worthwhile.

3   LOCATING OLDER PEOPLE IN TIME AND PLACE

In this chapter we consider the experience of ageing and old age in the context of the places and the times within which the older people in our study have lived their lives. How important to older people were the localities in which they lived? What were the salient events and experiences in their lives that they viewed as significant for their self-identity and well-being in old age?

To set the scene, we provide a brief description of the different localities within which the study was carried out.

Features of the study localities

Leeds: Woodhouse and Little London

Woodhouse and Little London – the catchment areas of the Caring Together group – form two distinct communities. They are similar in that they present a picture of inner-city decline, on the edge of the prosperous and bustling Leeds city centre. The proportion of households that are renting from the local authority is more than double the Leeds average (49 per cent compared to 21 per cent), and indicators of deprivation are considerably higher than the average for the city (for example, deaths from lung cancer are 139 per 100,000 compared to 69 per 100,000 for Leeds City). Over 70 per cent of older people interviewed lived in rented accommodation (mainly in the social rented sector), a reversal of the national picture.

Both neighbourhoods are rich in historical connections. Together, they formed part of the medieval manor of Woodhouse that covered a much larger geographical area than the locality which now bears the name. They have been described separately since the early nineteenth century.

Woodhouse

The current Woodhouse has clear, recognisable boundaries – contributing to, and reinforcing, the sense of a shared identity and shared interests. It spans out from both sides of Woodhouse Street and is

The streets of Woodhouse

bounded by distinctive geographical features, such as Woodhouse Ridge (an area of woodland and the site of earlier quarries) and Woodhouse Moor (old common land). Its present physical and social character has its origins in the early nineteenth century with the expansion of industry and manufacture. Mills and factories sprang up in the lower part of the area; and rows of back-to-back, terraced red-brick houses were built to accommodate workers and their families over the hilly area to the crest of Woodhouse Ridge. This new working-class development extended and reinforced the 'high street' character of Woodhouse Street, where people congregated around the pubs, shops and clubs. Quarry Mount School was built in the centre of the new development and remains a significant landmark in the area. St Mark's Church also dates from around this time, complementing the Methodist chapels, which were established in the later eighteenth century. In 1850, Samuel Smiles, the promoter of 'self-help', who lived on Woodhouse Cliff, laid the foundation stone of the Temperance Hall and the Mechanics Institute, which was largely built by the local people. This was the landscape that many of those interviewed recalled as the background to their childhood, youth and early family life. However, it mainly existed in memory, as a major redevelopment programme, started in the early 1930s and completed in the 1970s, substantially altered its character.

The first slum-clearance programme, begun in 1933, swept away many of the old courts. It was halted at the outbreak of the Second World War and then continued in fits and starts until the 1970s, when an extensive programme of wholesale redevelopment was proposed. The organisation of the local community to oppose and then to secure significant modification of the proposals was a key factor in maintaining continuity of residence, sustaining existing social networks and developing capacity for self-organisation. Several of the people interviewed were leading figures in this action.

Consequent on this housing development, many of the old street names were retained, although most of the street patterns disappeared. Woodhouse Street continued as the main arterial route through the area. Here are located the community centre, clubs, some of the pubs and the Methodist church, although most of the shops so vividly recalled by older people have gone. On one side of the street, running up to the Ridge, the traditional terraced houses remain intact, albeit some of them are in a poor state of repair. Many of the tall terraces have 'for let' signs, reflecting the encroachment into the area by private landlords to develop short-term lets for students. This has had a major impact on the social fabric of the locality, creating a transient population with limited investment in the area. What is noticeable walking around the neighbourhood is the absence of people on the streets during the day, in sharp contrast to the hustle and bustle of the city centre, a bus ride away. To the other side of the street and leading into Little London, there is extensive 1960s and 1970s low-rise concrete council housing, some of it designed for older people. The physical environment of Woodhouse therefore presents a very mixed and untidy picture and to the outsider displays many of the features of urban decay.

An examination of the archive of the Leeds evening newspaper for the first six months of the study during 2002 found 23 stories specifically about Woodhouse. These were fairly evenly split between positive reports relating to achievements and initiatives in schools and in developing community groups and negative reports about crime. Indeed, for older people living in the area, it was not fear of crime but an insecurity born of actual experience of crime that was the daily reality.

Little London

The few descriptions which exist of Little London in the late nineteenth and early twentieth centuries present it as a respectable working-class neighbourhood, with shops and churches focused around Camp Road.

Little London housing built during the 1950s and 1960s

In the experiences and memories of the older people interviewed in this study, however, little sense remains of a previously coherent community. Certainly, the geography of the area was less favourable to the conception of such a community. Woodhouse benefited from the focal nature of Woodhouse Street and its well-defined geographical boundaries; but Camp Road, which forms the main arterial road through Little London, flows into and merges with North Street leading into the city centre. Most significant, however, was the impact of the wholesale demolition and redevelopment of the area in the 1950s and 1960s. Unlike Woodhouse, where existing residents secured priority for the new housing, here people were rehoused into the area from similar clearance programmes elsewhere in Leeds. In addition to the loss of the old street patterns, much of the new development was based on tower blocks and flats. The new inner ring road cut through the area, while at Sheepscar there was a huge road junction; most existing churches were demolished. Moreover, the tower blocks in the main have failed to attract tenants who want to stay there and have been used increasingly to house a floating population of young people. Within the tower blocks, evidence of drug misuse is routine (e.g. syringes on the communal staircases). As in Woodhouse, fear of mugging and burglary reflects the likelihood of its occurrence. In recent years, there has been considerable regeneration activity, although older people in the area describe being left out of such developments as the focus has been on young people.

Within both localities – Woodhouse and Little London – the top three priorities for residents identified in the Community Plan were tackling crime (54 per cent), education (12 per cent) and improving the environment (7 per cent). During the course of the study, the area's future was the subject of contentious discussion because of plans for a large Public Private Finance Initiative (PPFI) housing project (subsequently rejected by tenants). The majority of those interviewed were directly affected by these developments, being tenants as opposed to owner-occupiers.

Hartlepool

From the early nineteenth century, Hartlepool was transformed from a small group of mainly fishing villages into a major industrial centre of the North East, based on shipbuilding, steelworks, textile

The seafront at Hartlepool

manufacture, brewing and, later, chemicals. At the same time, the development of the railways and its site on the North Sea coast made Hartlepool a major trading port for the North East and the West Riding of Yorkshire.

Whilst Hartlepool's industrial strength contributed to its prosperity in the nineteenth and early twentieth centuries, deindustrialisation over subsequent decades wrought havoc and decline, affecting one after another of its major sources of employment.

The First World War and its aftermath saw the destruction of most of the shipbuilding empire as local firms declined in number from 42 in its heyday to eight at the start of the Second World War, with a concomitant decline in the numbers employed. The Second World War saw a revival in the town's fortune as a shipbuilding centre and some 6,000 people were employed in the shipyards and engine works during and after the war. This temporary rise masked a deeper malaise and in the two decades following the war, closure and redundancies marked the lives of shipyard workers. By the early 1960s the last firm had gone into liquidation. Although some works continue, the numbers employed are counted in hundreds rather than thousands.

Linked with the shipbuilding industry were extensive iron- and steelworks, which experienced a similar process of decline though over a slightly longer timescale. From the mid-1970s, the British Steel Corporation pursued an accelerating programme of cutbacks that culminated in closure around 1980. Similarly, containerisation on the docks also contributed its share of redundancies. In early 1981, Hartlepool had, over several consecutive weeks, the highest proportion of unemployed in the United Kingdom.

This pattern of decline was evident in the experiences of the older men interviewed in the study. All of them had retired early, before the age of 65 years – linked with redundancy. Indeed, a number of the oldest men had experienced redundancy on more than one occasion, reflecting the different phases of deindustrialisation in the town's history. In marked contrast, the women interviewed who proceeded to the end of a statutory working life and beyond were employed in service occupations, such as care assistants, dinner ladies and home helps. For the children and grandchildren of these older people, remaining in the town tended to involve long periods of unemployment.

Although the Retired Resource Network focuses its campaigning activity on developments within the town, it draws its membership from the three wards of Rift House, Fens and Owton. Moreover, it is physically based within the community centre on the Owton Manor estate.

The wards present a very different physical and socio-economic profile. Rift House Ward comprises part of the Rift House and Foggy Furze areas. About a third is urban green space in the form of Stranton Cemetery, Rift House Recreation Ground and Brierton Lane allotments. Whilst most of the housing was council-owned during the 1960s, it is now mainly owner-occupied (93 per cent), a legacy of the sale of council housing during the 1980s. Fens Ward is almost entirely residential, consisting of most of the locality known as the Fens (except the Fens housing estate) and part of Owton Manor. Owton Ward covers the south western part of Hartlepool's built-up area. It consists of most of the housing estates of Owton Manor and Fens, respectively. Nearly two-thirds is council rented, in mainly older post-war estates. The unemployment rate here is over a fifth, nearly double the rate for the town as a whole and three times that of the other two wards.

RRN members are scattered over a large geographical area that is itself made up of distinct neighbourhoods. The streets in which they live are largely residential and well kept. Those from the Owton Manor area tend to live in semi-detached 1930s-built properties on the edge of the estate and are owner-occupiers in the main; many of those living on the newer former council estates have taken the opportunity to buy them from the council.

The significance of place

Older people live their lives within localities that have economic, social, environmental and spatial dimensions. The psychological dimension of localities, in terms of people's sense of attachment to, or exclusion from, the areas in which they live and those who live among them, is likely to have an impact on their life quality.

In exploring the significance of 'place', our starting point was to examine older people's own conceptions of the neighbourhoods or localities in which they lived. Localities may represent for older people a more important element of their sense of identity than would be the case for younger people (Scharf et al., 2002). First, there is length of residence in an area. People who have spent a large part of their lives within a particular locality are likely to have a strong sense of attachment to both home and place – however that is defined: immediate neighbourhood, street, ward (Phillipson et al., 2001). Second, as older people become less mobile, their immediate neighbourhood may constitute a large part of their social landscape, forming the spatial boundary within which most social life takes place.

There were important differences within and across the two study locations in the meaning and significance to older people of the places where they lived. In the discussion below, we examine the value placed by older people on features of home and neighbourhood and their relative importance over different phases of the ageing process. We also consider how older people from minority ethnic groups perceived growing old in the context of the experience of 'emigration'.

Attachment and belonging: Woodhouse and Hartlepool

Woodhouse (Leeds)

Generally, older people living in Woodhouse had either spent most of their adult lives in the area, having moved at the time of marriage or having been born and brought up within the neighbourhood. Their sense of identity was bound up with the place. Significant events and experiences over the life course were marked by physical features of the landscape.

I was born near St Mark's Church.

I was born in Woodhouse just down the road – you can see it from here.

My dad used to deliver coal around Woodhouse.

We lived in Woodhouse Lane … my grandma had a sweet shop and we all lived there and she used to make her own ice-cream and [sister] and I used to put about with our fingers.

I lived in that house for 35 years and my father and mother died there.

> I met my wife in the Quarry Mount Club ... it's still there but it's not a club now ... She used to go on the stage tap-dancing.

> I moved on to this estate when my daughter was a few months old. We usually go by her age *[to mark our time here]*.

Whilst people remarked on the enormous changes that had occurred to the physical fabric of the locality in their lifetime, there were also important elements of continuity reinforcing their attachment to the place. Memories of past lives were evoked by people and places in the present.

> We've seen a lot of changes ... student flats ... But I can look out the window and still see some of my old customers *[from working in a shop]* going up the road and remember those times.

For most people too, their sense of belonging was sustained and reinforced by the friends and neighbours that still remained and who provided continuity with previous life stages.

> What I remember are the streets of back-to-back houses – they're all pulled down now ... But there are still lots of friends that I know from the past. I wouldn't move away.

> Three of us – we all moved into the street the same time. We brought our children up together and we've grown old together.

Beyond neighbours and friends, there was a deeper sense of belonging in the extensive networks of acquaintances that provided a backdrop of support.

> I don't know all the names but I do know a lot of people to speak to that since my husband died have been great. People speak to me that I've never even known. They tell me they used to see me going about with my husband … he was always with me.

> Everybody's friendly in Woodhouse. 'Cos you know everybody – because you've known each other for such a long time … And its 'I haven't seen so and so for a long time – are they all right?' You're used to seeing them and having a chat with them … Everybody talks to you even in the bus queues … wherever you go.

Interest in, and caring about, acquaintances and neighbours was also reflected in the value attached to helping and being a 'good neighbour' that is discussed more fully in Chapters 5 and 6.

Shared memories of places, people and experiences during different stages over the life course provided a sense of continuity with the present and the basis for refashioning friendships in old age. Mrs Beddows described her relationship with others she had met through Caring Together, linking people and place in the following terms:

> I used to play badminton and all sorts of things in here [community centre] when I was 16 years old. It's like coming back home to your childhood days coming here to do things. We've a very close atmosphere between Woodhouse people.

This same theme is also illustrated in the focus group discussion with a group of seven women who lived most of their lives in Woodhouse and were now active in Caring Together:

Mrs Mattocks:	It's a boon is coming together on a Tuesday – we really look forward to that.
Q:	Did you all know each other before the group?
Mrs Beddows:	No – no – not really but we all lived close together.
Miss Jackman:	I did not know so many people. I knew Mrs Pelham through work.
Mrs Pelham:	She used to talk to me on the bus – general chat like.
Mrs Melville:	I used to see Mrs Bates at church.
Mrs Pelham:	I only know you as Mrs Bobby *[reference to the fact that Mrs Melville's husband was the local community policeman]*.
Mrs Melville:	I get that a lot – people come up to me at the Christmas party … and start talking to me … 'I knew Bobby'.
Mrs Pelham:	He was quite a local figure … and then Mrs Mattocks was always known by *[her maiden name]* – because of the fish shop *[the family owned a popular local business]* and Mrs Flowers was always the milkman's wife.
Mrs Mattocks:	Nearly everyone who comes to the party, I have served over the years at the fish shop.

The exchange also reveals another facet of life in the locality – the significant role played by those in the community who by virtue of their work not only knew a lot of people but were seen as linchpins within the area. Thus, Mr Ryman:

> My mother had a little shop – that was where you got to know all the gossip and who was doing what. Mum was that kind of person. She could stand and listen to someone's problems all day … If I didn't know people or my mum didn't, they knew me.

Woodhouse was perceived as more than a place to live. It was central to who people were; they were connected to others, both through their shared memories of landmarks, people and experiences and their reinforcement through ongoing contact with acquaintances, friends and neighbours. They described themselves as 'Woodhousers'. This included those who no longer lived within the physical boundaries of the area.

There were also a number of people who still identified with the locality on account of its links with their memories of growing up, going to school and courting, but they no longer felt connected to the place as it was now. Discontinuity of social relationships was a factor here, as illustrated by Mr Andrews:

> We had some fun as youngsters … My mother was born and died here … but I'm not sure I fit in here any more … I don't think I know anybody that I knew around in them days … There is nothing here for me.

For others, it was their perception of the chasm between Woodhouse in the past and in the present, especially the loss of mutuality and sharing in times of adversity, which was significant. Thus, for Mr and Mrs Murray, a couple who were restricted to their home, their narrative was replete with references to the places and people that shaped their lives but that now only existed in their memories.

Generally however, 'closeness' and 'neighbourliness' were regarded as distinctive features of Woodhouse people. Moreover, this did not only encompass 'Woodhousers'. A number of older people described themselves as 'newcomers', having lived in the area for less than 20 years. In common with Woodhouse people, they shared the values of reciprocity, neighbourliness and involvement and were active in the community and in Caring Together. It was these values – rooted in their experience of growing up in similar kinds of localities or having worked in similar kinds of jobs or involvement in the church – that formed the basis for their current engagement in the life of the area.

Strong themes of belonging and attachment sat side by side with concerns about the changed social environment of Woodhouse, in particular the level of vandalism and crime. Crime was not uncommon – around one in three of those interviewed had experienced theft, mugging or burglary within the previous year, a number on more than one occasion. Mrs Mitchell described the fear and anxiety that followed a recent burglary.

> I was asleep in my bed and he got in my bedroom window and went back the same way … It was a terrible experience. When I woke I realised he'd been in and I started shaking … the whole of my body … I'm afraid … I have not been able to go back to bed.

Mrs Mitchell now slept in her chair. Even so, the experience did not undermine her sense of belonging that was sustained through her attachment to the area, the support from friends and neighbours and the ties with the church that were a source of friendships over many years and a focus for valued activities.

Whilst these themes were reflected in the focus group discussion, what also emerged was the fact that safety and security assumed more importance in the context of people who felt less integrated into community life. Mrs Pelham recounted her plan to move out of the area to live nearer her daughter following two serious muggings.

Mrs Pelham: I've told people now – I'm leaving Woodhouse – I'm going to convince myself that's what I want to do.

Mrs Mattocks: I've been burgled three times but I couldn't go and leave my friends … no matter …

Mrs Pelham: No, I want to leave Leeds … I've nothing here.

Mrs Flowers: But your friends are here …

Mrs Pelham: But what do I see of you … I've a lot of people to visit but they don't always ask you back.

Hartlepool

The sense of belonging and attachment to place also emerged in the interviews with older people in Hartlepool. Generally, the focus of attachment was not to a specific locality as evidenced in Woodhouse but predominantly to the town and to the particular street or neighbourhood in which they lived. Here too, older people had spent most of their lives in the town. They spoke of it with affection, relating points of interest, history and new developments. While they might sometimes speak with a measure of self-deprecation about their town, there was a concern that outsiders should not do so.

Mr Edmonds: I have always lived in Hartlepool and I've always come back and I'm quite happy here. I know my way around ... I've worked in other places but I was happy to come home. I know what it is. It's never going to be a thriving metropolis.

Q: I am interested in that people have a sense of Hartlepool and doing things for older people in Hartlepool.

Miss Openshaw: Yes and I am proud of it. I think they see Hartlepool as having a pretty rotten reputation … The other day there was another article in the paper, slating, sneering at Hartlepool.

The town was the wider locale within which interest and/or leisure groups were located; where friends from previous life stages (school, work) with whom contact was still maintained might live; and a centre for shopping and meeting people. The street where the person lived or the immediate neighbourhood of a couple of streets was viewed as more familiar territory and the context within which neighbourly relationships existed in the sense of people keeping an eye out for each other or providing reciprocal help.

Mr Manning: My daughter says to me sometimes when we go down the road, 'do you know everybody?' I say: 'when you've been around for 75 years, you meet quite a few people'.

Mrs Manning: We lost the SRB [bid] because people around here took care of things.

Mr Manning: It did not ever look like a run-down area.

Mrs Manning: If it had looked run down we would probably have got it. We could have done with it because there was a lot of unemployment around at the time … especially in this area. But you see, people still kept their gardens nice, kept the houses, those that had bought them were all kept well. There are the council houses that were well looked after.

Mrs Gosden: This is great, around here. I mean I know I can just open my door and shout help and they'll come from all directions.

Memories of times past and links with the present spanned both the immediate neighbourhood and the town.

Whilst Mrs Jennings was notable for the range and extensiveness of her acquaintances and friends, the spatial pattern described, ranging from the street in which she lived to the town, was typical of many others.

> I have a couple of friends in the town that go right back to schooldays and some others that I still keep in touch with from work. There are still people around that I worked with and we went around together in groups – playing bowls, dancing, plenty of sporty things. We went down to Seaton together at weekends – so much going on. There are people in the groups I belong to – the RRN, the Friendship Group, a social group where we play whist and dominoes. I know people in the street here – some are good neighbours and we help each other out.

Mrs Adams described the process of becoming accepted within her immediate neighbourhood when she first moved there on marriage. Although she was now living in sheltered housing in another part of town, she retained contact with her former neighbours, whilst at the same time maintaining her sense of familiarity with, and link to, places in the town.

> I lived in a row of ten houses. My neighbours were very good and I had friends who lived elsewhere on the estate. I had moved to Owton Manor estate when I married – my husband came from there ... For a long time I didn't feel part of it – not being from the same area and they were very clannish ... I was 'missus' for a long time, never 'Eileen'. It was when my husband had his accident at work, they all rallied around ... one neighbour took me to the hospital, another looked after the children ... someone else ... and it went all the time he was sick

and after he died ... I honestly think – Harry was always there to give a hand to people around – that what I got from them was a thank you for what he did over the years ... When I moved into sheltered accommodation, people on the street gave me a card and a present ... I still see ex-neighbours ... I go into town most days ... I have a browse around on market days and I always go into the same place for coffee ... Some of us in the complex get the bus to the marina ... How it's changed!

Mrs Dobson described herself as Yorkshire by birth but Hartlepool by marriage, having arrived in West Hartlepool after the birth of her first child to the house she lived in until her recent move to sheltered accommodation. Relationships in the street were marked by a sense of neighbourliness, though this had altered in recent years as the houses changed hands.

I used to keep the nicest front of the house ... and did next door as well. I spoke to everybody ... And it was known you could come to my door if you wanted to know anything.

By the time she moved there was only one other 'neighbour' left – Moira – who arrived in the street about the same time as she had done. Mrs Dobson's decision to move to sheltered housing in another part of the town was precipitated by her house being burgled.

So I was glad to move here – but I still keep in touch with Moira and she says she'd like to move in here too.

For Mrs Dobson, though, the move did not cut her off from previous friends, it also opened up the possibility of forming new friendships with contemporaries who shared similar experiences of living and growing old in Hartlepool.

Convenience not attachment: Little London (Leeds)

For older people living in Little London, what was emphasised was the convenience of the location, its 'nearness to town', 'you can walk [to the supermarket] and there are plenty of buses'.

There was less sense of belonging in the way described above – no one, for example, referred to themself as a 'Little Londoner', although some had been born in the area and had lived there all their lives. Many people had moved into Little London relatively recently, including a number of those interviewed who had come to live in sheltered housing in the area. On the whole, residents here spoke of their attachment to home as opposed to the wider locality within which it was located.

Whilst there was a general sense of perceived poor quality of the physical and social environment of an area run down, people made a distinction between Little London as a place whose poor reputation they shared and the social environment of the immediate neighbourhood in which they lived. Mr Fleming, for example, was on first-name terms with most of his neighbours and described a pattern of practical and emotional support that he had come to rely on during his wife's illness and subsequent death and his own increasing disability. At the same time he expressed anger about the general state of disrepair of the area: windows blocked up as people moved out, communal areas unkempt and dirty, green spaces overgrown and his view of the housing department as 'putting anybody in to fill the place up'.

Others also spoke of their comfortable and quiet homes, but of external threats which disturbed them – crime and fears over personal safety, vandalism and graffiti.

There was a dissonance for some older people in their memories of the reputation of Little London when they had moved into the newly built estate and its current status. They spoke of their pride and delight at their modern homes and a lettings system that ensured it was 'respectable' people such as themselves who were housed there. In contrast, current tenants were seen as floating, unattached and a source of problems. A sense of isolation and threat within the tower blocks had led some people to move within the area to sheltered accommodation, or to move away altogether.

In summary, the meaning and significance of the localities in which older people lived varied considerably. For those who had a strong attachment to place, of primary importance was the extent to which people felt rooted in a locality, and where their perception of themselves was bound up with their relationships with people, particular places and experiences over key parts of their lives. Whilst it was evident to them that considerable changes had occurred in the social and physical environment of the locality, their continued sense of belonging was sustained through elements of continuity: shared memories and values, relationships with friends and neighbours, and familiarity of landscape – despite the outward physical signs of deterioration in the fabric of the place. Even so, attachment and belonging sat side by side with insecurity and threat from the external environment. For others who were less deeply rooted in particular places, their homes and the immediate physical and social environment of the neighbourhood were crucial in sustaining quality of life in old age.

Emigration and place

Among people interviewed from minority ethnic groups in Leeds (13), those from the Caribbean (eight) and South Asia (two) had moved to the locality within the previous 15 to 20 years. Most were now living in Little London. Those from the Caribbean had come to England as part of the big wave of emigration during the late 1950s and early 1960s, whereas those of South Asian origin had come later. They had all come to seek work or to join friends and family who had moved earlier. Mr Brown, an African-Caribbean man, described the choices available to him thus:

> In our case at home, we had no system *[to provide help to young people]*. You had to pull your socks up and had to go into scholastic work or into farming. You had to make the choice. You either had the brains and you got the job according to your ability or emigrate to America or to England.

The locality was not their first place of settlement on coming to Britain. On arrival, there was reliance by many on a network of friends and family that had come earlier: they clustered, therefore, in areas of pre-established communities within Leeds: Chapeltown, Hyde Park or the Blenheim area, on the perimeter of Woodhouse and Little London. They had moved into the district as the final step in a series of moves around the city.

Many of the stories of black and Asian migrants' experience on reaching the UK centred on their recollection of looking for work and the value attached to work – both important in shaping attitudes to retirement, as we consider later. The level of difficulty they experienced then still provoked anger and bitterness. In particular, those who had to take on less-skilled employment because their qualifications were not recognised still recalled their feelings of injustice and humiliation. Moreover, all those interviewed expressed a strong sense of duty and obligation to work hard. Mr Winston displayed the article written about him on his retirement after 35 years with the same firm, 'an unrivalled record of never once being late for work'. This had been achieved despite considerable ill health in the last seven years of his working life. His wife said:

> We came here as hard-working and independent people and when we came, this country could employ us and we look on that and we live contentedly. Fair enough, when he was poorly he could have retired early but we came here to work for our living and that is what we have done.

As with those in Little London generally, what was emphasised about the place was its location and accessibility to the city centre, especially in the context of getting older. But they also shared with others in the area a concern about the poor physical environment and the threat posed by drug dealing, crime and petty vandalism. A number of them, moreover, were actively involved in seeking improvements to their neighbourhoods. Mrs Brown, for example, was involved in the community association; Mrs Redding was a befriender with Caring Together and Mr King had formed a steel band with youngsters in the area.

There was, in a number of the interviews, some discussion about where people perceived 'home' to be. Recollections of 'home' as the place they had come from were couched in historical terms, with references to the traditions and cultural values of their youth.

In the interview with an African-Caribbean couple, these varied elements of 'home' were elaborated on, illustrating perceived ambiguities of the emigrant experience: that of both 'belonging' and 'not belonging':

Mr Brown: Well as they say 'to all the world I give my hand but my heart I give to my native land'. Home is always where you are born, where you belong.

Mrs Brown: You belong there you know, no one can say 'you shouldn't be there'. I know that they won't do it but they talk about repatriation – sending

> people back. That would not happen in your own native land – that is where you belong – your native land – because no one can say to you that you don't belong. But since my parents died, I don't think of where I come from as home so much. I have no one there now. I feel more at home here – I know it. I've lived here a long time. All my family are here, so this is my home now.

The death of parents and loss of family in their native land was a recurring theme in the way in which people defined their homeland. People spoke of sending money home to support elderly parents but feeling that their contacts had been cut when they died. Other people spoke of considering return but of having given up that idea with advancing age and ill health.

> I went back in 1978. I am not so much interested. When you are poorly, you want to keep yourself quiet, because a lot of people who are poorly they go back and they never come back. They die before they come back.

Only one person interviewed – an African woman – still retained close links with her homeland and with its traditional cultural values. She saw Nigeria as home.

> This is not my home. I took everything home in a short time, thinking I was going to die.

She planned to return to her native land to property she was building for her old age. She had also been going back every year for traditional healing which she found to be more effective than Western medicine.

Time: the impact of events and experiences on expectations and values

There were, in the narratives of older people in the study, specific key events or experiences that were either regarded as formative or marked a 'turning point', i.e. 'a time or event when one took a different direction from that in which one had been travelling' (Clausen, 1995). These reflected both the times through which they had lived – war, depression and boom – and their social situation, growing up in relative poverty within working-class communities where young people went to work aged 14 into jobs that reflected the local employment market. At the same time, the meaning of these events and experiences was different for men and women.

Opportunities and constraints

Most of those interviewed (apart from the younger 'old' and minority ethnic elders) described being directly affected by the Second World War. Most of the older men had served in the forces and their stories focused on the places they had been and how they had been changed by the experience. As survivors, there were conflicting themes of horror and excitement, of camaraderie and self-reliance, of loss and opportunities, which shaped their lives and the values they subsequently lived by. Mr Spencer described how his approach to life was profoundly affected:

> You learned not to care. You lost all reason of caring in a sense. You learned to take things as they came and not to accept authority.

Mr Melville recounted how his experience in the army had involved a major shift in occupation from going down the pit on leaving school at 14 to his subsequent career as a community policeman. The army offered Mr Gregory the taste of a different life, which was then disrupted on return home.

Mr Gregory: *[When I was called up]* I'd never been away from home. I'd never been anywhere and to get on a train and go right up to bloody Durham, that was summat strange to me. And then to go to Aldershot!

Q: Do you think it did you good.

Mr Gregory: Oh yes it did. I was in an Indian hospital in Burma you know. I learnt a lot, got to be a second-class nurse. When I came out of the army, I shouldn't have gone in tailoring, I should have taken up nursing. I could have been a State Registered Nurse.

For women, wartime both provided opportunities and disrupted dreams and plans. For young, single women in Woodhouse who joined the Land Army or the Wrens, it meant a break from the traditional occupations of women in the locality, tailoring and factory work, and opened up the possibility of a very different way of life. Mrs Myerscroft spoke vividly of the two years she spent in Paris as 'the most wonderful time of my life – I hated coming back'. For Mrs Evans, her period in the Land Army gave her a sense of freedom she never had before and set the seeds of a life ambition to have her own smallholding.

I would have stayed there. I loved it. I'd no intention of coming home but my father was ill so I came back to see him and as he was bedridden I stayed at home.

Her unrealised dream reflected both her sense of obligation to assume a caring role and the constraints imposed by personal circumstances and her social situation: marriage, children, marital breakdown and a life of struggle to support her family as a single parent. Even in old age, she still corresponded with a couple she had met whilst working on a farm, during the war.

The theme of missed opportunities marked Mrs Mattocks's narrative:

> Such an opportunity missed; all my opportunities were missed actually … I was training to be a hairdresser. Oh I loved it and I used to go down to Madame Boynton's down the road. It was 1 shilling and 6 pence for the three nights' training. She used to say to my Mama, 'your Edith is a natural' and I was. I used to do everybody's hair. I used to cut and do old-fashioned Marcel waving. And then the war came along and I couldn't do that. It was a ten-year apprenticeship and during the war you couldn't do it. You had to go into munitions. By the time the war was ended I was 21 and I thought it was too late to become a hairdresser. But I still carried on doing people's hair.

Young married women were left to manage as they could whilst husbands were away in the forces, either bringing up children alone or delaying plans for children. Mrs Coulter recounted the poverty and privations of war, managing alone for six years with two young children whilst her husband was in the navy: 'we struggled so we didn't go hungry'. Others spoke of the relationship difficulties they had to deal with at the war's end resulting from the very different experiences and expectations of men and women.

It was notable that the glimpses into the neighbourly structures of local communities that helped people to cope with the effects of war were predominantly women-centred.

A lot of the men were still away at the war. I used to help my friend Eileen. I used to sleep with her during the war because it was so hard for her with four children and I used to have two of them and she used to have two and we had to run through the brewery yard when the air raids went.

We return to this theme again in considering the experience of old age.

A powerful theme in the narratives of women was how their own lack of choice regarding schooling and work opportunities affected the value they attached to learning and education. At the same time, what also emerged was that even within families, opportunities (or the lack of them) were not equally distributed. Both these facets are evident in the accounts below.

Miss Goodman, 89 years at the time of our interview and the eldest of a family of seven, left school at 13 to go into service, despite being the only child in her village to get a scholarship to grammar school. She recalled her dilemma and feelings at the time:

My dad said 'I'm proud of you'. And I said to him: 'It's all right, I'm not going'. He said 'No!' 'No, dad', I said. Well, we didn't have a lot of money and being eldest I thought to myself that if I work I can help ... Later, one of my younger sisters also got a scholarship and she went on to be a head-teacher ... I've always been behind anybody to help them get what I didn't get.

Mrs Evans also got a scholarship to secondary school but instead of taking it up went to work in tailoring because her parents could not afford the uniform.

> That's the one thing I held against my mother ... If it was one of my other sisters then my mother would have made some effort to let them take it up. That's why I always vowed that no matter how hard it might be, if my daughter passed her 11+, she would go to secondary school ... and she did.

Like Mrs Evans, the high value attached to education by these women was reflected in their determination that their children should not miss out on the opportunities denied them. But it had another dimension as well: being a route into community activism built upon action for better schools when their children were growing up. Mrs Daltry described this in the following terms:

> I started working with the local schools ... I got involved with the school raising funds ... and then for a better education in the schools ... We never really got good quality teachers ... They'd just come here to do their year. The attitude was 'this was Woodhouse ... It didn't matter'. But I never thought it was all right for my children because I wanted something different for them ... Then I got involved in different things in the community ... tenants association.

Paradoxically, education was also the route out of the locality for children, with consequences for the structure and functioning of social networks for older people in the study (considered in Chapter 6). Mr Edmonds reflected:

> You see once they get academically qualified round here, there are no jobs for them, and then they move from the area. So this divides our family ... The only way they get the families to come back is if you are in business, like a solicitor and you are going to bring your daughter into a family firm, otherwise it is a move away.

In describing the pattern of their lives during early adult and middle years, what dominated in most men's accounts was work. For those in semi-skilled or unskilled work, the long hours, hard physical labour and relationships with workmates were central themes in their stories; for those few in professional occupations, work was a key source of status and meaning. These themes applied to both single and married men. Among married men, two broad patterns could be discerned relating to work and family life. First, there were those men who tended to maintain separate social and leisure interests from their wives, centred on workmates, sport and the social club. Mr Jones was typical in this respect:

Mr Jones: A group of us that worked together on the railways, we were in the bowls team – and I would go off to the football matches with mates … and we'd go for a few drinks together.

Mrs Jones: When he went off, I went to my ladies club … I was a joiner *[laughter]* – swimming, cycling club – I don't like to drink – I never did. So we did things separately.

Second, there were those whose interests were more couple-centred. Mr Perring described how he and his wife were both in a rambling club and spent much of their spare time walking in the countryside: they had also been active members of the community association.

Whilst women also worked, the pattern of employment was disrupted with marriage and children. Of those women interviewed in Leeds, most had worked in tailoring until children were born; later, as children went to school, many of them went back into part-time unskilled work – whether in factories, as cleaners, or as shop workers. Whilst the work pattern was similar for married women interviewed in Hartlepool, the range of occupations was wider and included such jobs as nursing, administration and clerical work. This reflected the more diverse social composition of interviewees in Hartlepool. Across the two localities, women were seen, and viewed themselves, as having the central responsibility for home and family.

For single men, their leisure time typically was spent with mates, predominantly in the social clubs or pubs. Single women, however, typically described a more extensive and richer social life as well as involvement in organisations such as church and interest groups.

These different experiences relating to work, leisure and family life have implications for managing retirement and ageing, as we see in later chapters.

Care giving and receiving

Among women generally, a recurring theme in the narratives of most of those interviewed was the extent to which reciprocal exchanges between family members extending to caring for older relatives – not just parents – dominated in their earlier years. This in part reflected the fact that, within these localities, the extended family of parents, aunts, uncles and cousins living in adjacent streets was a typical feature of their lives growing up and into middle age. Moreover, the currency of exchange was seen as having many different aspects which varied over time and with changing circumstances. These themes are illustrated in the following accounts.

When Mr and Mrs Tyson first married, they moved into his parents' house for the first couple of years – 'you couldn't get a house then'. Sometime after their first child was born, they moved into their own house, which they shared with his sister. When the children were young, Mrs Tyson looked after her mother who was in poor health and lived in a neighbouring street.

Mrs Tyson: I'd cook them their dinners and do the shopping.

Mr Tyson: And she did it for her auntie who lived in the same street who couldn't get out and another auntie who was also poorly and for my mam and dad. She used to go to the wash house three times a week with a big coach built pram full, piled high – three times a week – and wheel it back up again.

Mrs Tyson: When my mam died, my dad was at our house all the time so we went after a bigger house and he gave his up to move in with us. I was then going up with the kids one day a week to his mam and dad to do the bedrooms for them – that was to save his sister who went out to work – it was hard for her … It didn't bother me and I used to love doing ought for anybody – I still do.

Mrs Hyde's mother moved in with her when she was widowed, enabling her to go out to work part-time whilst her mother looked after the children.

Mrs Hyde: She used to keep an eye on the children. She had her own little cleaning job as well … until she was about 70.

Q: Did you care for her?

Mrs Hyde: No – she died quite quickly – she wasn't poorly for any length of time.

Mr and Mrs Kennedy moved to a house near where her mother lived, to be able to help out as she got older. This was seen to work well in so far as both parties were able to negotiate giving and receiving help with maintaining a valued lifestyle:

> She was very active ... treasurer of her old people's club ... She had a big operation when she was in her eighties – older than I am now and she just needed a bit more help so she came to live with me ... But all the time she really resented it. It's all right if you're healthy and you can do your bits and pieces and help out yourself ... And it used to be 'I'll go home and see if there are any letters' ... and we'd go and pick them up and go shopping. And then it was 'you go shopping and I'll stop here' because she wanted a couple of hours in her own home ... and then it was 'I'll stay the night' until she finally went back. Now then that was hard work for me because I had to go round breakfast, dinner, tea and bedtime. But it's what Mam wanted.

Whilst women were generally seen as being at the core of these caring relationships, unmarried men interviewed recounted how they had remained in the family home whilst parents got older and frailer. What was notable here, however, was that even in the context of them providing assistance to parents, mothers continued to retain control and responsibility for cooking and domestic routines: a pattern that was reproduced for the current generation of older women with adult sons at home, as we see later.

At the same time, whilst women expressed their espousal of the obligation to care, it was evident that the weight was not evenly distributed within families. Thus, for Mrs Evans, responsibility to care for her mother as she became frailer was deemed to be her primary responsibility, even though her sister lived in the next street.

I wasn't the eldest ... but next to the eldest. When my father was dying he told me, 'You look after your mum, because you're the only one who will'. And he knew whatever he asked me I would do.

In certain situations, however, other family members would share. Miss Marsh, for example, nursed her mother with whom she shared a house for some 30 years. Being in full-time work herself, she was helped by her sister-in-law:

I'd a very good sister-in-law – my brother's wife. She was marvellous. I was working in the school then. I would get up, light the fire, get her washed and give her a bit of breakfast before I went to school. My sister-in-law would come down about 9 a.m., give her lunch and stay with her until I got home about 4 p.m.

The strong ethos and value attached to caring continued into old age, although it was expressed in seemingly opposing ways. On the one hand, there was an emphasis on 'giving help to others', which found practical expression in 'neighbourliness', interest in and involvement in the community. On the other hand, there was a vociferous rejection of such expectations of their own children and an expressed anxiety not to be a burden to them. We consider these dichotomies in more detail in subsequent chapters.

Summary

Place – in the sense of the localities in which people lived – assumed enormous importance in the lives of older people in the study. This reflected not only length of residence and familiarity with the area, although that was part of it; it also related to the extent to which people's sense of identity was rooted in the physical and social landscape they inhabited.

The two geographical areas covered by Caring Together – Woodhouse and Little London – have many common features and, to the outside observer, display many of the characteristics of inner-city decline: poorly maintained Victorian terraces in multi-occupation, tall tower blocks, shops boarded up, abandoned open spaces and the experience of crime a reality for a significant proportion of older people. Even so, these localities were perceived very differently by older people living within them. For those living in Woodhouse, there was a general sense of being part of a community to which they felt a strong attachment. For those who had lived most of their lives in the area, significant life events and experiences were connected in their memory with physical and social features of the place. Continuity of friends and acquaintances over time provided the link between the past and the present, solidifying and reinforcing people's sense of belonging. Even among those who were not personally known to each other, being able to compare stories of their linkages with people and places they each knew contributed to their perception of being part of a community. Strongly held values of mutuality, 'looking out for each other' and neighbourliness were common themes in people's narratives and extended to those who were relative newcomers to the area. Older people expressed an investment in the locality and did not want to leave: it was part of who and what they were. For those living in Little London, although people generally did not subscribe to being part of a community that embraced the locality, they made a distinction between the immediate neighbourhood, street or close in which they lived and where neighbourly relationships were maintained, and the wider area whose poor reputation they shared.

For older people in Hartlepool, the focus of attachment to place was twofold. First, they identified themselves as Hartlepool people – familiar with its physiognomy and history – whilst also recognising its social heterogeneity. Second, there was the immediate neighbourhood of a street or couple of streets where reciprocal exchange was valued. It was notable here that moves within the town, for example into sheltered housing, appeared less disruptive of social relationships. In part, this was because of its comparatively small size, which meant that one could meet up with previous neighbours and friends; and in part, because it was possible to establish some connection with people in the new setting, for example through a mutual acquaintance or having gone to the same school.

For older people from minority ethnic communities – all first-generation emigrants – their conception of 'home' had a dual meaning. On the one hand, it was bound up in the cultural norms and values of their childhood and the family they had left behind in the 'old country'. On the other, it represented the lives they had built and the families they had reared in the 'new country'. But whilst some also expressed a certain lack of security in their acceptance in the 'new', the death of their own parents also represented a break with the 'old'. Some of them, moreover, were also involved in community action – part of constructing a better life for themselves and others.

In seeking to locate older people's lives in a wider socio-historical context, what emerged were several strands that connected individual experiences, family, socio-economic circumstances and life chances, and major social events such as war and depression. For older people in this study, most of whom grew up in relative poverty and whose lives were marked by war, what dominated in their accounts were alternating themes of opportunity and constraint, struggle and hardship, and care giving and receiving within both the extended family and the wider community. These themes, which also have a specific gender dimension, were central in shaping their life histories and core values. They provide the backdrop to understanding both the varied resources available to older people in dealing with ageing and the strategies they developed for managing the process.

4 TRANSITION AND CONTINUITY

In order to examine diversity and change over the ageing process, the study included older people across four decades – from those approaching 60 years to those in their tenth decade. In this chapter, we describe key transitions and changes in the lives of older people in the study, and the meaning and significance they attached to them. Invariably what shaped their approach to managing the changes accompanying ageing was a set of values that both gave meaning to their lives and influenced the kind of strategies they adopted to make sense of their experiences. At the outset, therefore, we set the scene by considering the values that underpinned people's sense of well-being.

Underpinning values

Caring: giving and receiving

As we noted in Chapter 3, for most people interviewed, themes of caring for and caring about dominated in their stories over different stages of the life course. This was expressed in the importance attached to 'neighbourliness', in their descriptions of how they looked out for each other, their stories of mutual assistance in times of adversity and the reciprocal exchange of little kindnesses that were a routine part of daily life. Men and women equally were part of, and contributed to, this neighbourly exchange. Additionally, a recurring theme in the narratives of women, in particular, was the extent to which reciprocal support between family members, extending to caring for older relatives, was a feature of their early and middle years, even though the currency of exchange and the flow varied over time.

The strong ethos and value attached to caring continued into old age, although it was expressed in seemingly contradictory ways. On the one hand, there was vociferous rejection of any obligation on children to look after them in old age and an expressed anxiety not to be a burden. On the other hand, there was an emphasis on 'helping others', which found practical expression in the value attached to 'other-centredness' – both 'neighbourliness' and community participation.

Not being a burden

Although caring for older relatives had taken up a major part of their lives, older people were adamant they did not expect their own children to care for them. This was graphically expressed in the following exchange in a focus group of mainly active older people in Hartlepool.

Q:	Would you expect your children to look after you?
	[All – loud 'no']
Mrs Pearson:	I've told my daughter that if I get incapable, she should shove me in a home.
Mrs Manning:	None of us want to be a burden on our families do we?
Mr Jones:	They've got their own lives to lead – their social lives and their work.

Q: Did you feel when you were caring for parents and relatives that they were a burden on you then?

Mrs Manning: No way – but it was different then – families lived in each other's houses – parents, aunts, grandparents – whereas now they don't ... and they were there to do the necessary if the mother wanted to go out.

Mrs Hyde: Not that we don't help out *[laughter]* but the thing is we want to go out ourselves and do our own thing.

Mrs Manning: We're a very considerate age group actually aren't we!

[General agreement and laughter]

Similar themes emerged from both the individual and focus group interviews in Leeds:

> I wouldn't have my sons at home with me all the time and they couldn't live with me ... You love them and that but you couldn't live with them.

> I had my mam and dad all those years but much as I loved them they choked me. I want my own doorstep – I wouldn't want my daughter to look after me.

> They want to do their own thing, don't they?

Older people's rejection of the obligation on children to care for parents stemmed from their own desire not to be a burden and the view that children had their own lives to lead.

Your family have got families – you can't be dependent on them.

I've never been one to hang on to someone else.

For some older people, their determination not 'to be a burden' also found expression in the emphasis they placed on taking care of their own health and well-being.

When you're getting older, you've got to look after yourself to make it so that other people don't have to look after you. Otherwise, if you're silly about things then somebody has to look after you. And if you're sensible, you can look after yourself.

I'm so frightened of being a nuisance. I wouldn't risk anything because there is no one belonging to me here.

How older people reconciled not being a burden with having to accept help is partly explained by the importance of another key value, namely, reciprocity.

Relationships based on reciprocity

A pervasive theme across all the interviews was the significance attached to reciprocity in social relationships. Whilst the nature of the exchange which Mrs Kennedy (83 years) recounts below was specific to her, the sentiments were shared across the localities:

I help *[family who live locally]*. I help them. I used to do the babysitting. Now I have to go out and cut their lawn. I've just painted their garden gate – the son doesn't have time. He does work for me if I need him. I won't get up on the stepladder any more. It's not fair to my son, that's going to have to suffer by looking after me.

Miss Goodman was both a giver and receiver of help and support through Caring Together. Although becoming increasingly frail, she was a major contributor of cakes and scones for the parties and fêtes:

> It's absolutely wonderful because you get to help out. Maggie brought me along a befriender – a student. I taught her how to cook. Although she's gone home, she still writes to me.

Where older people did require considerable help, like Mrs Evans below, acceptance nevertheless involved difficult choices and negotiations that were underpinned by mutual acknowledgement of the significance of maintaining some equivalence in the exchange. Not only did this enhance self-esteem and self-worth, but it made acceptance of help legitimate.

Like many other of her contemporaries Mrs Evans left school at 14 to work in tailoring. Married with a child in her early twenties, she brought her up alone following separation from her husband. She described a 'hard life', maintaining several jobs at the same time (cook, cleaner); it was 'a struggle to survive' and to give her daughter what she did not have – 'an education'. She also cared for her mother living nearby when she could no longer manage: 'I just took it in my stride'.

Now in her late seventies, osteoarthritis had crippled Mrs Evans. She walked with increasing difficulty with the aid of sticks, in constant pain. Even so, she struggled to reconcile her need for help with her sense of what was appropriate to ask of her family.

It's hard being worn ... wearing out ... but at the same time the life I had made me self-reliant and independent – that's what's so hard about being as I am ... My daughter gets angry with me because she says I don't let her do enough for me now. But I always say to her, 'I didn't want you to have a life like I had' ... My son-in-law is very good – anything that he thinks is helping me ... I never ask, he's always there for me. He got me a second-hand wheelchair. I made him take the money. We had a fight over it.

'Other-centredness': social engagement and neighbourliness

Across both localities, people expressed a strong sense of 'other-centredness'. This had two aspects. First, there was the sense of being part of, and belonging to, something that was bigger than oneself or one's immediate family. This ranged from an interest in, or concern about, others – 'I haven't seen you about ... are you all right?' – to being involved in social action to make things better 'for people in the area'. Second, there was the value placed on being a 'good' neighbour, from keeping an eye out for others to doing a 'good turn' for them.

We now turn to consider those points of transition and change over the ageing process and the meaning they had for older people in the study.

Transition to retirement

For everyone in the study – men and women – retirement marked a key transition in the life course. This applied equally to those not in paid employment but whose spouse or partner was retiring. The point at which this happened, however, was variable. Whilst, for many, it occurred at the statutory age of 60 or 65 years, for a significant minority it came earlier (because of ill health, caring obligations or redundancy) or later (where choice and opportunity extended paid working life). The context in which retirement occurred was decisive in terms of the meaning attached to it.

Leaving early

Where retirement was brought forward by factory/industry closure and large-scale redundancies, as for men interviewed in Hartlepool, it was generally welcomed at the time: everyone was in the same boat, they were coming to the end of what they saw as a hard working life, and they were in a better position than younger people who faced unemployment or at least a struggle to stay in work. For some, too, work-based relationships were sustained subsequently through involvement in unemployment centres and/or community groups. Others embraced redundancy/early retirement as a chance to begin a new phase of life and leave what had become an intolerable work situation. In both types of circumstances, the primary concern of all those leaving early was not the loss of paid work, but whether they could manage financially.

Q: Was retirement a wrench for you?

Mr Jones: Not really ... It felt with everything closing down, everyone was going ... At 63, I was quite happy to finish ... but well before, there was a little niggle in the back of your mind, 'Am I doing the right thing and can we manage' ... we worked it all out, didn't we *[turning to his wife]?*

Mrs Jones: Oh ya, it was a joint decision.

Where retirement was precipitated by ill health, however, the sense of loss evoked was compounded by the suddenness of the life change and the reassessment of oneself as no longer 'active'.

> I was active, very active. I worked until midnight on the night before I went into hospital for my operation. When they told me I wouldn't be able to go back to work, it was a bolt from the blue. It was as bad as being ill, not working.

Staying on

If some people retired early, there were also those who continued in paid work until a time more of their choosing. Mrs Jones, above, whose husband took early retirement, decided she would continue as a teaching assistant in the local primary school, because of the pleasure she got from work.

Mrs Jones: I decided to stay on *[working]*. It was only a couple of hours a day ... It was fun. I really enjoyed it ... I loved the children.

Mr Jones: And I stuck the hoover in my hand.

Mrs Jones: And you learned to wash up too.

She eventually left at the age of 70 when staff changes meant she would be working with new people. Miss Mills finally left work at the age of 67 with retirement being thrust upon her when the factory closed: mixed up with her sense of loss of a job she enjoyed were concerns about managing on her own:

> Well I wouldn't have retired then but ... I mean you couldn't get a job at that age. I might have got one as a

cleaner. I didn't want to do that and I thought I'll manage on what I've got, because I could get my pension. Sometimes it has been very much of a struggle, but when my sister died, she left me a little money. So now I never have to think where the next penny is coming from.

Mrs Pearson similarly left her job as a receptionist at 62, 'past retirement age', partly to care for her husband who was ill. When he died, she worked for a couple of hours as a dinner lady because 'I just loved working'. Now in her seventies, she talked with regret at having to leave work:

I loved going out to work. I still would go out to work but I mean when you talk about looking for a job or anything they look at you as if you are daft. Nobody's going to employ you at my age. I enjoyed going to work and meeting people. Really offering services to people – it wasn't just going out to do a job of work. It was actually providing a service because you were the first port of call for anybody's problems whatever they had, in their home lives or whatever. You were the first person they spoke with, so it was quite interesting.

Thus, some of those who were reluctant to retire did manage to get other jobs – women in particular often took on part-time work as shop assistants, dinner ladies and cleaners. Miss Goodman got work in the university canteen – and expressed considerable pride at the fact that she stayed on until the age of 79! What was notable also was that she developed an entirely new set of friends, considerably younger than herself, who ten years on provided considerable practical and emotional support. One of the few people in the study in a professional job went back doing the same work on a part-time basis. He had become ill following retirement, because as far as he was concerned he had lost what gave his life meaning.

Retiring 'on time'

For many of those interviewed, retirement, when it came at the end of a statutory working life, was welcomed. In part this reflected the kind of work they did: factory work in particular was felt as hard and gruelling. Some had struggled with ill health in the latter years of their working life and collapsed into retirement with a sigh of relief. Mr Winston, an African-Caribbean man who had spent 34 years in a small engineering factory, expressed it thus.

Mr Winston: Well I enjoyed work but it was hard but you had to stick at it. At the end I was poorly because the work was rough but now it's easier so we do not inherit the easy part.

Q: So were you pleased to retire?

Mr Winston: I not pleased to retire, I glad to retire. I should have retired about six years before, you know, but my doctor told me that I could still go to work when I was poorly. I made a bad mistake because I shouldn't have gone back to work. I had to lift my legs to go up the stairs but I managed to bear it out.

For Mrs Franklin retirement offered both release from repetitive work and time for herself. Although she had regular contact with her immediate family, her joy was grounded primarily in the strength of her spiritual life:

Now I'm retired I enjoy my life. Somebody said, 'Do you feel lonely?' I said, 'Loneliness is a thing of the mind, my dear'. I don't intend to be lonely. When I get up, I like to have the place clean. I try to clean it the best I can. Sometimes, I can't do it well. Sometimes I watch television. I've got videos … I've got books … That one

> it says 'Fear Allah and control the Tongue' … it tells you if someone comes and says something about someone, control the tongue.

Others disliked their work and were happy to leave. Miss Jackman, although she had to give up her car, was delighted to be able to devote more time to the things she enjoyed doing:

> I hated cleaning. I used to work full time and believe me it was a hard slog. I was working in sewing *[before that]* and then I couldn't get a job and that was the only job I could do. They were very good and they bought me all sorts when I retired but …

> Yes I hated it. I have never ever thought what can I do today – I still don't. Every moment of my life is filled. I'm happy now.

> I didn't realise how wonderful it would be. I'm free for the first time in years. I do what I want. All the duties and things to do and all the rest and I had enough.

Whilst Miss Jackman was somewhat atypical in her overwhelming joy at retiring, the sense of freedom she described was echoed in many of the interviews. Even where people were ambivalent or cautious about leaving work, they considered that a new period of their lives was opening up which they had to 'work at' if they were to make best use of it.

Working at retirement

Most people described a conscious decision to 'work at retirement'. There were apocryphal or cautionary tales about people they knew or whom they had heard about who died shortly after leaving work because they had given up.

I'm of the belief that if you don't use it you'll lose it. So I'm trying to learn all the time. I don't believe in giving up. I believe you should use your allotted span as much as you can because if you don't … Many people … are sort of rushed out rather than wear out because they just stop and they say that's it, 'I'm not going to do anything'.

Bound up with the idea of working at retirement was that this phase of their lives opened out opportunities to pursue new interests and expand their learning:

I joined a woodwork class … I've done bookcases, coffee tables … and I learned to swim for the first time.

I did a course on computers … I've always been interested in figures … I've an active mind that way.

I didn't have a chance to be educated … Now I grab all I can to continue the education I missed out on.

Couples who had up to then maintained relatively separate interests had considered what they could do together. For some, this was also a chance to broaden their circle of friends and acquaintances.

We did our own things … I still did my voluntary work with the Red Cross … but we decided to take up bowling together.

We liked dancing when we were younger so we thought that would be something we would both enjoy, so we joined … we were both on the committee there for a while as well.

I said to an old friend, 'we've decided we should do something together now … we should start a new life. What are we going to do with the rest of our lives?' So she said 'Why don't you join our dance'. So along we went and we've been in that ever since.

For others, it meant they could spend time with each other.

Q: What was it you were looking forward to *[when you retired]*?

Mr Rowlands: Being with Ellen *[his wife]*.

Q: Did you have activities you wanted to pursue?

Mr Rowlands: We used to go out twice a week, my wife didn't drink, we used to go for a meal and to go to the theatre, Playhouse or somewhere like that. She enjoyed that … We went on holidays abroad for the first time.

Yet others described a pattern of different and parallel lives in retirement that gave rise to some tension. Until she finished paid work, Mrs Hyde's life had centred on home and family. When she retired she became involved in action to regenerate a community centre, broadening her circle of friends in the process. Not only did she develop in confidence – 'I wouldn't open my mouth in company, I was a shy, quiet little soul' – but she also learned new skills such as word processing and using a computer. Her husband described feeling like a widower at times, separated by her involvement; his interests and activity were home-based: music and being 'the family taxi-driver'.

For a number of people, plans and aspirations for retirement were thwarted by the onset of chronic ill health – whether their own or their spouse's – at or near the point of leaving work.

Mr Perring was somewhat ambivalent about retirement – 'I loved my work' – but he and his wife were actively planning to reverse what had been their work/leisure balance: long-time interests in walking and community work were to be brought centre stage. However, Mrs Perring suffered the first of a series of strokes. As she became increasingly disabled and her husband assumed more of the caring and household tasks, their social and physical space narrowed and contracted. Short walks in the countryside or in the park took the place of hill walking for a time, until that too was impossible; a move out of the locality to accommodation that was more suitable for her needs took them away from the organisations they had been involved in and 'I didn't feel like starting again'. By the time his wife died some 14 years on, Mr Perring's own health had deteriorated and he had lost contact with friends.

The work goes on

The idea of working at retirement was not a one-off event but an ongoing process. Where people experienced difficulties on account of ill health and disability, they sought ways of continuing to pursue the things that interested them, even if this involved some adaptation in the form of the activity. For example:

> We had the car and I was driving until I was about 70 ... and we went on regular days out ... and even when we got rid of the car, we still continued to travel around – but then by bus and train – all around West and North Yorkshire.

> I got myself a piano and did some refresher courses ... Someone said could you accompany tea dances ... so I went along to see ... I learned the repertoire ... And I got to just love it ... I got interested then in all kinds of

dance … I can't do that now … But I do go along to the exercise group, though I cope now by faking it!

Similarly, patterns established in the years post-retirement could undergo radical change (as for example, with the death of a spouse), both positive and negative. We consider this in more detail below.

Bereavement

Most of the older people in the study had experienced loss through the death of someone close to them. Whilst the meaning of the bereavement depended on the nature of the loss and the quality of the relationship with the dead person, how they dealt with it and its impact on their lives in old age depended on when it occurred and the other things that were happening to them at the same time.

Timing

Around half of those interviewed on a one-to-one basis had lost a spouse and several of the unmarried women had lost a significant lifelong friend. For more than a third of them, however, the death had happened in middle age. Forging a life without a partner for them was not a problem that newly emerged in older age: the bereavement was managed in the context of bringing up children, coping financially and developing interests and friendships as a single person. For Mrs Gratton, widowed in her forties, the impact of the bereavement was felt acutely in her middle years – bringing up teenage children alone, managing work and family and making ends meet. She was persuaded by a friend to join the Widows Association at the time, and this both helped her to get out socially and meet new people and stimulated her interest in getting involved in campaigning around older people's issues later. Mr Edmonds similarly, whilst having to adjust to life without a partner, was still working and in good health at the time and had friends who could encourage him to go out.

It did appear, however, that resolution at one point in time was not necessarily final. In the context of other changes occurring in later life, such as ill health of friends, family or self, the acute grief felt at the time of death could be experienced anew.

In the case of a further quarter of those widowed, the death occurred shortly after retirement. Although they felt cheated and bereft, those people who had retained/developed interests and friendships on giving up paid work described how these offered both a resource in managing the bereavement and a basis for getting out and about as a single person. Mrs Kennedy, widowed within a couple of years of retiring, explained it thus:

> We were very involved in the bowls club together ... When he died I could have sat at home and just cried and that's all I felt I wanted to do ... But the people at the club ... said 'you need company, come with us' ... And that helped me ... And I've developed a lot more since I lost him ... I had to ... It's hard to be a person on your own ... because you've gone through everything the two of you. You don't truthfully have very much of your own mind ... and you're having to work out all the problems on your own ... But I took on things I wouldn't have dreamed of doing.

Mrs Jennings similarly described working at forging a new life following her husband's death:

> We always went together. We did everything together more or less ... He was a good talker ... He'd always conversed with people and he could get on with anybody. After he died, I thought well I can't sit in the house and

do nothing and talk to myself, so I thought I'll see what is going on round and about. So that's why I joined the Friendship Group and I joined the RRN and then just over a year ago I started going up to the residential home ... for a chat and to play whist. It gets me out into company. It's a bit of time to yourself that you enjoy.

For women, particularly those whose lives centred on family and domestic routines, the death of a spouse could expand social relationships and activities. A number of those active in community organisations had got involved for the first time in their seventies, following bereavement. Others spoke of renewing old friendship ties, loosened over the years.

I've known *[friend]* for over 50 years and it's sort of come around in a circle ... We've come back together again like when we were younger.

Key to this renewal was the availability of opportunities – places to meet people with whom one shared common interests and experiences and encouragement to get involved. It was notable, for example, that the locality focus of Caring Together, the diverse forums and activities it had established and the varying levels of involvement that were part of its functioning, drew in and enabled older people to flourish.

Mrs Ismay: It was the best thing I ever did when I joined there *[Caring Together]* and it was my sister-in-law ... She said to me why don't you join the community centre – they have all sorts of things going off. So I called one Friday and ... that was it.

Q: Was this since you husband died?

Mrs Ismay: Yes I think he'd been dead about a year when I went and joined. But yes I look forward to the Tuesday group … I wouldn't miss it.

Some required more support, however. Mr Rowlands, whose wife died of cancer, went along to a regular 'comfort group' at the hospice. Being able to help others in a similar position, whilst also deriving support himself, gave him the confidence 'to get on with my life'. He was able to resume interests he had shared with his wife – trips to the theatre, days out – although now within the framework of the Caring Together group.

Even where the death of a spouse opened up new opportunities, it also brought with it a profound sense of loss, particularly the loss of intimacy:

Mrs Mattock: It's being alone isn't it … It's at night when you shut the curtains.

Mrs Pelham: Yes you look round and you think … I'm on my own now. I feel very much alone sometimes. I don't exactly feel lonely but conscious of the fact that I'm on my own.

Mrs Flowers: Yes I do. I've a lot of friends but they can't be there all the time can they?

And,

Being on your own after being married for 50 years … The children have moved away and the link isn't strong enough: they have their own lives to lead.

Cumulative loss

For those in advanced old age, what was remarked upon was that death – of relatives, friends, and neighbours – was occurring at ever shorter intervals.

> There's not many of the old friends left … We just went to another funeral last week … There's only a few now of the old workmates left … There was another friend a while ago … and my sister before that.

Here too, it was the experience of accumulated loss – of family and friends – that contributed to a sense of social isolation.

> I had three sisters and a brother. They are all gone. Everybody's gone and they were all younger than I am. My husband had four sisters – they're all gone.

For a number of people, longevity had meant they experienced the death of an adult child. The resultant persistent grief and emotional distress in part reflected the fact that this was 'not the right way round': it was 'out of time'. Mrs Dobson, in her tenth decade, made the point that although she had a comfortable life she would not want to 'bury another daughter'. Death of an adult child also reinforced a profound sense of isolation and emptiness for which there was no clear substitute.

> It's worse to lose them than even your husband, I think. It was bad when my husband died nearly 25 years ago but then for my son to die when he was only 48, it was terrible, terrible, so sudden as well. I was with him at dinnertime and it happened at teatime. I still haven't got over it. It comes to me many, many times. I think about him because he cared a lot about me and if I didn't see him every week, he'd ring me up two or three times a

week and I did see him a lot, whereas all that's finished more or less. Well it is finished.

Later bereavement in the context of declining health also had a profound impact and meant that it was more difficult to deal with it. Miss Goodman expressed not only sorrow and loss following the death of her lifelong friend, with whom she had shared everything, but a sense that despite having many friends, there was no one on whom she could rely just to be there for her.

> I've lost my friend. I'm on my own and I'm so frightened of being a nuisance because with having nobody – like I was there for her and she was there for me. Its very strange now because *[with other people]* you're a bit on your guard and you've got your hand up like this *[stretches her hand out from her body, palm facing the interviewer]*. It's like because you're here and I'm talking to you, I wouldn't like you to think I was trying to hook on to you.

Miss Mills (90 years), similarly, talked of the death of her closest friend. Whilst she had lots of people she was friendly with, as well as half a dozen she regarded as 'true' friends, she considered that 'friends that you can share your memories with' became increasingly difficult to make as you got older (although as we see in Chapter 6, where shared interests brought people together, some did develop new, close relationships in late old age).

Keeping well and managing ill health

For everyone, the process of ageing brought with it a deep consciousness and awareness of body and mind. This applied as much to those who regarded themselves as in 'good health' as those who experienced restrictions on account of ill health and disability.

Awareness of body and mind was manifested in different ways. There was the view that you could not take your body for granted any more as you did when you were younger. It could also let you down unexpectedly (and for those who had experienced a sudden, life-threatening illness such as a heart attack, there was an acute appreciation of this).

> When you're older you have to listen to your body more.

> When you're younger, you can get away with things but you can't as you get older. Like lifting things … if I lift things the wrong way now, I can do myself an injury.

> Your body deteriorates as you are getting older – eyesight, hearing. You get more conscious of what you can do and what you can't do.

But alongside awareness of body and mind was the realisation that one had to work to keep well and keep going, a topic we now turn to.

Healthy minds and bodies

A strong theme across all of the interviews was the need to look after oneself positively: maintaining a healthy diet with regular hot meals, eating fresh fruit and vegetables, and getting fresh air. One focus group of older women considered the relative benefits of alternative remedies and therapies to keep well, drawing on their own experience of use. Others emphasised the importance of exercise – whether this was taking part in exercise groups, walking to the shops or, for those who were less mobile, walking about the house, dusting and polishing.

Since I got old I am trying to keep well.

When you are younger, you can get away with it. When you get old you have to work at it.

My daughter says to take it easy and sit down … I have two legs. I don't want to be lazy. When God takes me I want to be fit!

Keeping well was about enjoying life, having fun and having people with whom one could share laughter and enjoyment.

Well, you think, you've passed that age of having to do things. You are going to do things that you enjoy. That's part of life at this stage. It's just enjoying life.

"It's just enjoying life"

I like a good laugh and letting my hair down. Others say to me, 'Why don't you act your age?' I have lots of aches and pains and stuff wrong with me but I try not to let it get me down.

I always feel better in myself, when I can get out, meet people and have a laugh. It makes you feel better in yourself.

Everyone, without exception, stressed the need to work at keeping the mind active. Indeed, for those who were restricted by physical disabilities, 'keeping the brain going' assumed enormous importance. People across the age spectrum talked about exercising the brain: doing crosswords, puzzles and reading.

Mrs Wilson regularly counted backwards from 100; Mrs Long, who had been an office worker/bookkeeper, whiled away the time at the GP's surgery by translating pamphlets into shorthand in her head. Whilst mental stimulation was seen as essential to well-being, it was evident also that exercising the mind was a positive strategy to keep dementia – the condition most feared by older people in the study – at bay.

Pushing yourself

Keeping well was also about 'not giving in' and 'pushing yourself to do things'.

> I sit here and think I won't bother going to the shops and then I'll think get up ... You've got to make yourself go, haven't you!

> We've all got problems but you have to overcome them. If you gave in to your problems, you wouldn't get out of bed or you would sit around in your home and want somebody waiting on you all the time. I hope that doesn't happen to me for a long time, because once that comes, you've lost your quality of life ... You are just existing then as I look at it.

> I tell myself, 'Come on! Shake your feathers, Janet. Get up and get on with it.'

> Letting up is giving up.

The tenor of people's comments, particularly those of the 'younger old' suggested that 'pushing yourself' had the character of a moral imperative – it was something you had to do. Some people they knew just gave up – and giving up was giving in to ageing.

I'm not sat away like a lot of these seniors do. They think 'I'm getting too old' and they'll sit in their living room all day. To me, you need to be out and keep going like a young person until you are not able to do it.

Some of the 'older old' shared similar views. Thus, Miss Mills:

Q: Do you think of yourself as old?

Miss Mills: Only when I'm moving ... I couldn't run if someone was coming after me, so to speak. But I've got a young outlook. I'm interested in history and geography and I like people ... I think if you read and watch things ... I've always been observant, you keep young that way ... There are others – there's a lady upstairs who's been here 13 years and never been downstairs *[laughter]* and another who just sits all day in the common room and says she hasn't been outdoors for three years.

Q: And is she fit?

Miss Mills: Oh yes. She walks a jolly sight better than I do. It's that they haven't any interest. You can be brain dead though you're still alive. Well, it isn't going to happen to me.

'Pushing oneself' and 'not giving up' presented considerable dilemmas for people. If people slowed down, did that mean that they were giving up? Mrs Bates, in her eighties and actively involved in community activities, presented the problem thus:

You don't think 'I'm getting old' and in a way you want to be the way you were. But I also want people to know that there is change taking place – but that I still can be

> part of things ... There needs to be some acknowledgement that we are getting old ... but that at the same time, we're not past it.

The perceived conflict was not only experienced in relation to their individual life choices. It also reflected their view of how others saw old age, and their determination not to be 'old' in the sense of being passive, uninterested, pathetic, unloved and unloving.

There were those who had established a relatively comfortable relationship with their bodies. For them, letting go a little was acceptable, and indeed it was viewed as an appropriate way of dealing with the loss of energy they experienced.

Miss Openshaw, for example, planned activities in advance to use her energy more effectively and to cope with pain and immobility:

> I have what I call my 'no' days, when you are not up to doing anything ... I try to plan each day so that I have no more than one thing to do and then I pace myself.

Others also talked of pacing themselves, taking it easy and taking it slow:

> At one time we used to waltz through the cleaning. Now it takes us the best part of two days.

> I do a bit and then I sit ... I've nowt to grumble at.

Yet others prioritised the things that were important and that they could still do:

> There are certain things I can't do which I will give up. But things that I can do, I try to do. Because once you start thinking: 'I've retired now. I'm giving everything up' ... That's the downward slope.

Managing ill health

Health – or its absence – was a major preoccupation of older people in the study. This is hardly surprising given that national surveys indicate that around half of those over 65 years report their health to be 'less than good', rising to two-thirds of those over 75 years; moreover, whilst fewer than a quarter of 'young old' people (those between 65 and 74 years) report levels of disability that impinge on their ability to carry out activities of everyday living, such as personal care, housework and shopping, this applies to three-quarters of those in advanced age, i.e. over 85 years (Arber and Cooper, 1999).

Here, most of those interviewed, including the very active, experienced at least one chronic health problem. The emphasis in their stories, however, was not on symptoms of ill health. Rather, their focus was on the extent to which they were able to maintain valued social activities, interests and relationships.

> Health – that dictates what I do in life. I say that because it is the state of my health that stops me from doing things.

> Not being well … means you can't do the things you want to get on with … I don't worry about being ill … everyone gets ill … I worry about not being able to get out, about not being able to go to the shops or do what I have to do … see my friends.

Conversely, when people were in poor health, what they talked about were the changes that had occurred in their lives as a consequence. Thus, for Mrs Yardley, problems with her bladder meant she did not trust going out any more with friends. For others, declining health had led to a reduction in social contacts and social relationships.

For those experiencing ill health or disability, there was a shift in emphasis, reflected also in the language used – from 'keeping well' to 'coping' with ill health. As ill health or disability began to circumscribe what older people could do, they sought to sustain, at some level, those interests and activities that were valued. Miss Beeching and her friend, who were passionate about walking and nature, had sought other forms of expression for their interests when declining mobility had curtailed their trips: they now went out on day trips, using the bus instead of walking. Mr Fleming, unable to go out alone, retained a lively interest in community affairs and was a prolific letter writer to relevant council departments about the problems in the local area, e.g. litter and vandalism. Mr Cartwright had decided to reduce some of his committee engagements 'to have a bit of time for myself', but had taken on additional work as a chaplain in a nursing home.

Generally, managing ill health was about coming to terms and dealing with a combination of problems, whose impact was not only cumulative, but sapping of personal and social resources to cope with them. Difficult personal choices had to be made by individuals. Mr Ryman, a severely disabled younger man, spoke bitterly about having little life at all. Although he was not so disabled that he could not go out independently, the considerable pain he experienced meant that for him it was a question of balancing his need for company with how much pain he was prepared to tolerate, in a context where the social life of his 'mates' revolved around the pub and there was no one who came to see him.

Ageing: joy, ambivalence, acceptance and despair

'Flowering' of old age

Key transitions and experiences that were a part of the ageing process had the potential to usher in new opportunities that for many of the older people in our study represented the 'flowering of ageing'. Among those actively involved in community groups and in our partner groups, a recurring, major theme was not only the sense of purpose and value such involvement offered, but the felt experience of being part of something that was bigger than their personal interests and concerns. For Mrs Wade, the networks she developed through her activity in the RRN were extensive and wide-ranging and her work consumed a considerable part of her day-to-day life and interests.

For others, however, side by side with this sense of 'being connected' was having time and space to oneself, the 'freedom' to enjoy life and the lifting of the burden of responsibility. It was women in the main, however, who relished their 'liberation' from the routines and responsibilities imposed on them by the demands of spouse and family. Some like Mrs Beddows, who had become active in Caring Together, articulated a clear sense of joy at having an identity separate from homemaking, family rearing and working.

> I used to go to work part-time and then go home; take the children to school in the morning, home, make the dinner and then the husband's tea. I didn't have a spare minute. I used to think to myself 'Oh wouldn't it be lovely just to have a few minutes to spare for myself'. Now you can't just believe it … that you are your own boss … that you can do what you want … make your meal at your own time.

Mrs Melville, a long-time community activist, revelled in her continued involvement in community activities through Caring Together, but with the knowledge that she could choose what to do, that there were workers who could take on the day-to-day tasks.

For others, like Miss Emsley, being old was a positive time in one's life.

> You can't know until you've been there what it's like to be old. They say 'well, you've had your innings' ... But it's the other way round. We've got over the rough unpleasant stuff – jobs, family, whatever – and now is our chance. But they don't see that. You can't until you're old yourself see how precious every day is ... now is the time to get to enjoy yourself.

Ill health and disability were not only problems to be managed, but represented potential threats to well-being, in so far as they reduced or impeded people's ability to be involved, engaged and able to continue doing the kinds of things they enjoyed or were of interest to them. For those who experienced difficulties on account of ill health or disability, the process of ageing was presented in more ambiguous terms.

Struggle for balance/equilibrium

The dominant response reflected an ongoing struggle for balance or equilibrium. Whilst acknowledging the losses they had experienced and the need to reorient themselves to focus on things they could still enjoy, they nevertheless at times railed against being old and/or disabled, albeit their sense of being old had only made its presence felt on account of the disability. For Miss Marsh and Miss Coghill, old age had 'crept up' on them and was revealed in the difference between their memories of what they used to do and their current situation:

> I used to jump on a bus and do everything for myself. I never thought about getting old.

> I'd go walking and all sorts of things … get on a bus and go different places.

For older people here, their presentation of themselves as 'content' or 'not grumbling' or 'not being a moaner' was interspersed with a frustration with their declining health. This duality was typified in the following:

> I don't feel my age you know … *[and later in the interview]* The thing that annoys me is my sight … I do so miss going out … and then I tell myself 'stop it', be thankful that you can do what you can do … You've got to fight *[getting old]* … many a time I could sit down and cry … if I could see I could do such and such and then I put my mind to it and I've thought well I've had some happiness and I haven't had much illness.

This is illustrative of another common theme, namely that people's assessment of well-being not only related to the here and now but encompassed an evaluation of themselves over the life course. This was expressed positively by Mrs Nuttall, following an exchange with the interviewer (one of the older people from Caring Together, also from the locality) when they recalled past events, places and people:

> You sometimes wonder where all the years have gone. And then when you talk about what has happened, there's an awful lot gone into those years.

People's striving to maintain some kind of balance was sorely tested in the face of an accumulation of adverse events, following one on the heels of another. Mrs Coulter (85), on the cusp of being confined to her own home, described her life as a constant struggle: 'I had a very hard life, love. I've had to cope with one thing and another all my life'. Even so, her more recent experiences – death of her husband, ill health, loss of mobility, her friend's admission to care and her daughter's serious illness – tried her ability to cope:

> Things keep throwing me back ... then I start to get climbing again.

Acceptance

For a number of people, their response to ageing and disability was acceptance. Mrs Winston, for example, described how her life had been dominated by helping others and now:

> It is my time ... I have to give thanks every day for the return I am getting for helping others. When I first heard about this cancer I was very worried ... but I can tell you I am travelling happily because of all the love, care and affection that I get.

Similarly, Mrs Franklin:

> I try to be positive and hope that nothing will happen to me and if it does there's nothing I can do about it. My mother used to say to me, 'Learn to be satisfied with what you've got. Learn to settle for what you can afford'.

Among those African-Caribbean elders suffering ill health and disability, all of them articulated a strong, explicit invocation of God as an explanation of their acceptance of their situation.

My life has been built on the word of God and put into practice. It has helped me all along life. It helps me now in my pain.

Mr Brown remarked that he had lived his allotted span of 'three score years and ten'.

Among some of the very old, acceptance reflected in part the value of a life well lived. But it also related to the fact that there was joy in living.

For a small number, however, acceptance appeared to reflect the fact that if life was a 'bummer' in old age, what could one expect? Mr Andrews, for example, who indicated he had no friends and had lost contact with his family, commented:

I've just realised I'm an old man now … and when you're old, you don't have fun … I've stopped having fun. It just doesn't bother me. I'm quite happy. I'm not miserable. I'm quite pleased with myself really.

Anger and/or despair

For a small number of people in the study, their response to their situation was anger and despair. For Mr Fleming it was the abrupt loss of everything he had valued with the sudden onset of a major disability, the pain provoked by the loss and the lack of support/resources to change things.

There's nothing for disabled people around this area … All of the things I enjoyed doing, I can't do them any more … gardening … we [wife and self] used to be in a walking club … swimming … going to cricket and football matches … but they don't cater for a lot of people in wheelchairs … I begged and begged at the hospital for them to put me to sleep … It broke my heart. It's the evenings that are the worst. I lock all the doors and I don't see anybody walking about.

Mrs Varley also expressed anger and grief at the discontinuity between her previous active life and the restrictions imposed both by her recent ill health and the demands of the medical regimen. Now, when she did go out, it was to the hospital for one of her numerous outpatient appointments and investigations.

I'm young at heart ... I only went grey a couple of years ago ... These last couple of years though I'm a dead loss ... I've never been one to hang on to anyone ... and now look at me.

For others, like Mrs Nunn, there was a more profound and deep-seated sense of loss that was reinforced and exacerbated in old age, but had not newly emerged then.

I've always had to look after myself and do things for myself. And now I get irritated because little things I could do for myself, I can't do ... I manage ... I have to manage. You just reconcile yourself to knowing that you're not going to do anything or go anywhere ... I got very depressed last year ... I began to worry – I was forgetting things ... We all say that here – we worry when you just can't get a name sometimes and it can worry and worry you.

For Miss Madden too, her sense of loss and despair had developed over time. Her story was dominated by the experience of caring for her brother from late middle age, after he had suffered a stroke. Then she 'was a prisoner in the house' on account of her caring responsibilities; now she still felt she was a prisoner because 'I have no one to go out with and nowhere to go. I daren't go out'.

Summary

People's responses to the transitions that occurred over the ageing process were shaped by their experiences and values, formed over the life course. The central and underpinning value carried through into old age was that of interdependence – that tied together seemingly contradictory notions of caring about others, not being a burden and an emphasis on reciprocity in relationships.

For many older people, the transitions that accompanied ageing presented opportunities and possibilities. The sense of the 'flowering of old age', of the possibility (and actuality) of growth and development, was described in vivid terms by many of the older people in our study. For many of them too, it was their involvement in our partner groups that opened up opportunities for optimising gains in old age. For others, it was the range of interests they had begun to pursue following retirement (and bereavement) that also extended their circle of friends and acquaintances that were most important.

There were, however, circumstances in which older people's conception of their lives as being filled with opportunities was challenged and where their capacity for adaptation was stretched to the limit. First, there was the acceleration of loss in advanced old age, a process that was also accompanied by a depletion of resources available to deal with it. Second, there were situations in which the sudden onset of ill health and disability, impacting on both their sense of themselves and their ability to do things from which they had derived pleasure, led to a profound discontinuity between their past and present lives. Third, there were also individuals for whom life had dealt a poor hand: the ageing process was simply an exacerbation and extension of that – with the difference that the poor hand they had been dealt meant they had less in the way of resources (friends, family) to draw upon in managing the process.

One of the facets of ageing described by older people was increasing awareness of mind and body. They 'worked at' keeping well. Moreover, the language used – 'pushing yourself', 'not letting yourself go', 'not giving up' – expressed the hard work involved. Whatever their chronological age, people made a distinction between 'being old' in the sense of giving in or not being interested in the world around them and acknowledging that they might need to pace themselves. The weight of time – measured in years lived – did not mean that one was *past* living and loving.

Most people then, including those who experienced some restrictions on their lives as a result of ill health, disability or even the tiredness and lack of energy described by those of advanced years, sought to adapt to the changes that occurred in ways that enabled them to find continued meaning, pleasure and stimulation. Whatever strategies they adopted, at their core was the need to maintain an active mind and body. It would be too simplistic, however, to conceive of the process of adaptation as smooth and unproblematic. Whilst for some it was expressed in this way, for most it was couched in terms of an ongoing struggle for equilibrium that alternately gave rise to feelings of anger, despair and acceptance.

Finally, whilst older people demonstrated considerable capacity to manage the challenges of ageing, adaptation did not occur in a neutral environment. First, they were continually confronted with, and reproached by, attitudes and behaviour that devalued ageing and which they had also internalised. Second, individual circumstances and events within their own life history influenced the resources that were available to them in adapting to loss. These issues are explored further in subsequent chapters.

5 THE EXPERIENCE OF EVERYDAY LIFE

In this chapter, we focus on the everyday experience of older people's lives and the shifts and changes that occurred as people moved into advanced age. What was life like for older people on a day-to-day basis? What were the things that were important to them and gave pleasure and meaning?

In organising the discussion, we have found it useful to categorise the sample into two broad groups that we have described as 'out and about' and 'restricted'. These are no more than descriptive categories. Their particular meaning for the older people in the study is set out below. What was evident from the analysis was that the pattern of people's day-to-day lives and the opportunities available to them were shaped and constrained by the extent to which they were able – for whatever reason – to get out and about independently. Key questions of interest, then, were how and in what ways people's sense of well-being was sustained when they lived their lives within the confines of their homes or immediate neighbourhoods. What was it that made for a good life when they could no longer get out and about? Alternatively, was it essential for well-being in older age that people's physical and social worlds were not constricted within narrow spaces? An exploration of these questions would, we felt, give insight into service needs and priorities across the spectrum of older age.

'Out and about'

More than half those interviewed on a one-to-one basis (48) were characterised as 'out and about', i.e. on most days, during the day, they spent some time outside the home. This 'out and about' activity spanned a diverse range: trips to the shops and socialising with friends, neighbours and family; engaging in hobbies and leisure pursuits; involvement in community and other interest groups. People in this group were generally younger than those who were unable to get about much on their own. Even so, they did vary considerably in terms of age (a quarter were over 80), health status and personal circumstances (see Appendix, Table A13). We describe below the different patterns of 'out and about' life found within our study, under the following broad headings: an 'ordinary life', 'downsizing', a 'sociable' life, a 'busy' life, and 'working for the community'.

Maintaining an 'ordinary life'

These were older people who had since retirement established and maintained a gentle rhythm of life within a social world comprising family, neighbours and acquaintances/friends. For them, the key difference post-retirement was that the structure of their day was no longer organised by, or centred on, work. Mr Gregory reflected this pattern. Aged 77, he was born and lived all his life in Woodhouse. He came from a large family: two of his sisters still lived in neighbouring streets and his only child, a daughter, was married with a grown-up family within a 20-minute bus ride from his home. His wife had died some ten years prior to his retirement from the tailoring industry. His daughter subsequently taught him to cook and he had looked after himself independently since then. His only concession to age was 'to slow down a bit' in doing his household tasks: 'I clean one room

one day and do another room another day and then I do my landing
... I go off to the laundrette another day'.

Although he had experienced several serious health crises in recent years, Mr Gregory had maintained a pattern of life that had a daily and weekly rhythm: he got up early at the same time every morning; went out for a stroll and picked up his newspaper; called in to see his sisters most afternoons. He did 'a fair bit of walking now during the day', but fear of being mugged meant 'you daren't go out at night'. He was also a voracious reader. Once a week, he visited his daughter and went to the social club to meet friends for a drink at Sunday lunchtime. Mr Gregory was on first-name terms with lots of people in the locality and knew most by sight 'to say hello'. He did shopping for an elderly neighbour once a week, though 'I don't go in' the house, and also took on the little jobs she needed doing. A member of Caring Together, he was an enthusiastic participant in fundraising/social events such as the jumble sales, fairs and the annual party. He was comfortable with his life though he expressed concern about the future:

> I've had my downs. I've had my bad parts ... But I've had a good life really when you come to think of it. I've had a good life. If I can go and see my daughter and see she's all right, that makes my day.

> I'm managing just at present but I don't know how long it will go on for, because I've been getting a lot of pain lately ... And I keep going to the hospital for check-ups.

Downsizing

The term 'downsizing' refers to the approach of those older people whose social life had contracted due to ill health or disability or the loss of close friends, but who placed a high value on going out and keeping active.

For these people, changes and adjustments had been made to the pattern of their day-to-day lives over the ageing process. Miss Mills (90) had been a keen hill walker and rambler from youth into early old age. Now, although she had experienced mobility problems over several years, she walked every day into town from Little London:

> I can manage to walk there and back. I go more for the exercise than anything else ... I don't want to get like a pudding really.

Her brother and sister had died close together but her nephew visited from America once a year. Miss Mills knew a lot of people in the area, although a number of her closest friends had either died or moved away in recent years. A sociable lady, who enjoyed the company of others, she tended now to avoid large groups on account of her hearing difficulties. However, she made her own way to the small social group run by Caring Together once a week and was also visited at home by a befriender from the group – a young woman whose company and conversation she found stimulating. Living on her own, she enjoyed her own company:

> I don't want to live with anybody now. I'd rather be on my own. You can do what you like; have what you like; say what you like. I'm not selfish. I've looked after other people and it's my turn now.

Similarly, like many others interviewed, she rejected the term 'old' and set high store in keeping up with hobbies and maintaining interest in what was happening in the locality and in the wider world:

> I've a young outlook ... I'm interested in history and geography ... I read. I knit ... If you haven't an interest,

you can be brain dead even when you're alive. Well, it isn't going to happen to me *[lots of laughter]*.

Mr and Mrs Tyson (83 and 77 respectively) centred their day-to-day life on family, home and trips out and about. Both suffered from chronic, serious ill health, including respiratory and heart problems. Mrs Tyson's closest friend from school days had died some years before; she and her husband had formed one half of a foursome with the Tysons, and they had spent a lot of time together. Now, the Tysons spent most of their time together as a couple: although both were well known in the neighbourhood and were 'friendly with everyone', they had no 'close friends'.

With us getting older, you feel as though you're closer and you think every day's a bonus.

Household tasks, cleaning and small shopping were shared within an established daily routine. A couple of times a week, they took the bus out to the countryside or neighbouring towns, the 'pleasure trips'; another day they went also by bus to visit a daughter some miles distant, with Mrs Tyson baking a cake for the occasion and perhaps picking up bits and pieces of shopping their daughter might need. Out on the street and in the bus queues 'you always meet people you know to have a chat with'. A strongly held value on 'helping others' found expression in the regular 'little turns' they did for a neighbour.

A 'sociable' life

A third pattern within this 'out and about' category encompassed those older people who maintained a very active social life within extensive networks of family and friends. Mrs Allen's experience is illustrative. Widowed in early middle age, Mrs Allen (78) had moved into sheltered housing from her home on the Owton Manor estate some years previously. Having suffered a stroke, she had little use of one arm and some mobility difficulties. Her two sons were both married and lived relatively near. Mrs Allen maintained relationships with friends she had made on the estate where she had lived since her marriage: she regularly went back there, although her best friend, 'my soulmate', had died. She had stayed friends with her son's former mother-in-law and they regularly spent Sundays together. She had made new friends in the sheltered housing complex: a group of them took little trips together, went out for a meal or watched the bowls. She had met them through the activities organised in the unit: coffee mornings and whist drives. She saw her sons and their families on a weekly basis: 'I bake pastries to take with me – they like my baking'. Outings with friends were interspersed with trips to town: part of her weekly routine was browsing and shopping on market day.

> I'm out doing something or with someone every day except one when I stay in to do my cleaning … I have a full life … I don't have much time to watch TV … but I prefer anyway to sit down with a good book.

Like many other people in the study, maintaining her personal appearance was very important to her and she had the hairdresser come to her once a week.

A 'busy' life

There was, among these 'out and abouters', a group of older people who had on retirement gone out to develop new interests, hobbies and leisure pursuits. Freed from the responsibility of work and family, they saw this phase of their life as one of expansion of opportunities: not just in terms of activities, but of making new friends.

Miss Emsley (83) described a busy, full life centred on hobbies, leisure and social activities, although their form had changed somewhat as she'd got older. Her closest friend had died some years before, shortly after she had moved from London to live in Leeds. She had no close family but a lot of friends and acquaintances in different parts of the country through her different interests (though not people she described as very close or intimate friends).

Her main hobby was breeding and showing cats. Although she no longer competed, she spent most weekends at shows, clubs and meetings around the country, either as a judge, spectator or participant: 'it's very strenuous but very satisfying – not only because of my love of cats but socially it's a very important part of my life'. Miss Emsley was also a 'passionate gardener – growing things, swapping seeds, plants and cuttings' with neighbours and friends. She also went swimming once a week and considered there were things she still wanted to learn.

Although she had not lived long in the locality (nine years), Miss Emsley had become active in Caring Together. The different kinds of activities she got to do there (crafts and exercise group) were a source of stimulation and brought her into contact with people in the locality – 'everyone is friendly' – reinforcing her sense of belonging. Once a week she went along to the exercise group, seen as a substitute for a long-time interest in dance, which had become impossible on account of arthritis, although 'I miss the dancing most of all'.

Like Miss Emsley, Mrs Kennedy (84) had wide-ranging interests and diverse social networks, based on her hobbies and leisure pursuits: bowling, Red Cross, crafts, gardening. Most days were spent out and about; weekends often involved driving to different parts of the country to play in tournaments. This contrasted with her period in life when her children were growing up:

> Then all my life consisted of was going to work, cleaning the house, my husband did the garden and I looked after the children. I just lived at home ... Now I travel all over, playing in competitions ... Once you get a bowl in your hands and you are on the green, there's nothing else in your mind except that green and what's at the other end and you must just enjoy what you are doing and forget anything else that is troubling you for a couple of hours. It is really very, very restful, very good for you truthfully.

> Last weekend I went to Paisley to play bowls – Saturday and Sunday ... I don't think I have any more energy than anybody else. I just enjoy doing ... My grandchildren sit around more than I do ... If there was something I didn't enjoy doing, I wouldn't want to do it.

A number of people interviewed had developed strong friendships in later life that expanded their interests and social activities. Mrs Kovac and Mrs Markham, both aged 78 years, spent a lot of time together. Mrs Kovac had been widowed for over 20 years and her only child – a son – had moved to Scotland some 16 years previously. Mrs Markham was divorced and had brought up her children alone since her youngest was three years old. Each of her three children lived in the city but she saw only one of them regularly. Mrs Kovac, since retiring as a machinist, had learned to swim and had also taken up woodwork. Although living in the same sheltered housing complex, they had only met three years before at a day centre. Their friendship extended their social life and leisure pursuits: once a week, they went along to a craft group; another day, they went to the cinema together; and they were planning to take up t'ai chi: 'there's only one day that we're not occupied'. They no longer went to the day centre because 'we've more important things to do with our time'. Mrs Kovac had also got to know Mrs Markham's daughter, who either visited them once a week, or they went together to the daughter's house for tea.

Mrs Manning and Mrs Hyde's friendship had blossomed when they both got involved in the local community centre some years before, although they were acquainted prior to that from living in the same locality. Whilst both were very family oriented, they also went out together, for instance, bowling a couple of times a week.

Working for the community

A distinctive characteristic of many of the older people in our study was their other-centredness. The high value they placed on 'helping others' found further expression in their active engagement in community groups and campaigns geared to 'making things better', not only for immediate friends and neighbours, but also 'for the community'. RRN members were strongly motivated by a desire to make things better for others.

Mrs Grattan: Yes and to get your point of view over to different places where you've got to have a loophole to get into. If you have to go and have a battle with the council or something, if you have got a group like that, you can go forward.

Q: So it's more than just meeting other people, it's about getting things done?

Mrs Grattan: Oh yes and trying to make a better community for the older people, which is what I think was the idea behind it all.

For a number of people, their involvement in community activities as they got older was an extension of a lifelong participation in civic and religious groups – both at the local level and in broader arenas. Miss Jackman (73) and Mrs Bates (81), for example, were active members of the local chapel. Miss Jackman, for as long as she could remember, had been involved in both the religious and social aspects of chapel life. Thus, she had run the youth club for many years and had become a member of the management committee of Caring Together (albeit reluctantly) through the chapel – 'I didn't think I was clever enough'. Mrs Bates was also a regular church-goer and 'friendly visitor', visiting church members who were ill or confined to the home. However, her involvement in Caring Together had only occurred following her husband's death a couple of years previously – 'he didn't really like going out'. Now she participated at every level of Caring Together – social activities, fundraising and volunteer group and latterly in the research group. Mrs Kennedy's involvement in the RRN (she was a relatively recent recruit) reflected her outward focus. She felt she had a lot to offer, and it still rankled that she was regarded as 'too old' to continue as a first aid trainer with the Red Cross, something she had done for many years. Mrs Melville's (73) focus now on working for older people was an extension of her campaigning activity within the local community. She wanted the experience and capacity gained over years, which had made 'a difference to a lot of people's lives' and had 'created a lovely community spirit', to be sustained as a resource for people growing older. For Mr Cartwright (72), his personal experience of caring for his wife with a severe disability had extended to involvement with carers groups and thence to engagement with working groups developing policy and practice in respect of carers in the city. Both Mrs Daltry (70) and Mrs Wade (63) were actively involved in community action far beyond their immediate localities. For others, responsibilities of work, home and family had meant that their engagement now in working for the community had newly emerged since retirement and/or bereavement of a spouse. For many of them, it was an outlet for their considerable creative energy and was rooted in their own experience of hardship.

Restricted

Although the term 'restricted' is cumbersome, we have used it in preference to 'housebound'. Many of the people in this category did get out of their homes, but only with help: they were unable – for different reasons – to get out and about independently. At the same time, some of those who did not venture far beyond their homes or immediate neighbourhoods felt constrained, not by physical disability, but by mental health problems or the fact that they were socially isolated.

In the discussion below, we explore the different circumstances that contributed to people's 'restriction' in the sense defined above and examine the pattern of their daily lives. We then consider those factors that sustained, contributed to, or adversely affected the well-being of these older people.

Life on a narrow stage: restricted to the neighbourhood

There were 21 older people in this category, just over a third of whom were 85 years and older (see Appendix, Table A14 for a profile). These older people (and they were the second largest number in the sample) had as a distinguishing feature the fact that they still managed to get out of the house independently, although they did not venture far beyond their immediate neighbourhood.

We can discern four different patterns of circumstances contributing to the experience of restriction among older people within this group:

- gradual deterioration in abilities reflecting concurrent problems of ill health and loss of mobility

- onset of ill health and acute hospital admission

- change in lifestyle

- social isolation.

Gradual deterioration

Eleven of the 21 older people in this category had over several years experienced a gradual contraction in their spatial worlds. Whereas at one time the pattern of their day-to-day life was similar to that of people in the 'out and about' group, now day-to-day life was conducted on the narrower stage of the local area or immediate neighbourhood, because of their restricted mobility. With the exception of one couple, all were women. Musculoskeletal problems, such as arthritis, were the main factors contributing to poor mobility but chronic health conditions like diabetes, angina and respiratory and circulatory difficulties also featured.

There were several common themes in the narratives of these older people: continued involvement in the tasks of day-to-day living; negotiating needed help in ways that retained some form of equivalence in the exchange; making active choices about what things to sustain and what to let go; seeking to keep up with social activities and friendships for companionship, fun and sharing memories. Additionally, it was evident that long-term residence in a locality maintained continuity of social relationships: friends carried through from earlier periods in life were a source of emotional and social support in the face of restriction.

With increasing disability, Mrs Evans (78) shared the household tasks with her daughter who lived nearby:

> I make the bed and vac downstairs ... my daughter does upstairs ... I dust and polish the bedroom furniture, she changes the bed linen ... and she does the shopping.

Mrs Evans's son-in-law did any odd jobs that needed doing and her grandson went with her to collect her pension, 'since I was mugged'.

Mrs Evans used to go shopping with her daughter and son-in-law; then she went along and sat in the café while they shopped; now she gave them the shopping list to do it for her – 'it got too much. I also do my washing and ironing as little as possible because I can't stand for long ... and I'm a bit doddery hanging washing out'. She continued to attend the weekly club at Caring Together, taking a taxi the short distance. Many of the friends she had known throughout her life met there: 'If it wasn't for Caring Together, I'd be a real mope-head ... miserable'. She also maintained daily social contact by telephone with friends who were similarly restricted. Another friend from chapel visited every week.

Mrs Peters (94) placed a high value on having opportunities to socialise and get out of the house. She went to the day centre once a week and tried to get out most days to the local shops, although failing sight and poor mobility contributed to her fear of falling:

> I sit here and think: I won't bother going and then I'll say to myself: 'Get up' – you've got to make yourself go.

Speaking to one of the older interviewers, they shared stories of people they both knew in the locality. Miss Etherington (87) similarly derived pleasure from her monthly outing with friends and her weekly trip to the luncheon club. Most other days she was content to look out of the window and see people she knew going by. Miss Beeching sought to continue with her church responsibilities, which provided a point of social reference and a sense of purpose despite being quite restricted:

Miss Beeching: If my leg's bad, I can't always get up to chapel you know …

Q: So do you like to get up there every week?

Miss Beeching: Saturdays, coffee morning on Saturday and sometimes it's my coffee morning like next Saturday I help out Jean. She helps me when it's my coffee morning but I go other Saturdays as well. The same on the rota, we have a cup of tea every Sunday after service so I'm on the rota for that and for the flowers.

Traumatic life events/onset of acute episode of ill health

There were a number of older people whose sense of themselves as active and independent had been challenged starkly and suddenly. This occurred as a result of specific events and/or losses happening together or following on from each other. Some, moreover, were on the cusp of transition into being restricted to the home. Mrs Mitchell (82) was traumatised by a burglary of her house as she slept: the shock had exacerbated her poor health. Whilst friends and family had rallied around to support her, she had (temporarily) tipped over into a very restricted life at interview. Mrs Myerscroft's (89) recent ill health and acute hospital admission (she had fallen and lain on the ground for several hours), alongside the sudden death of a good neighbour, had drawn her back into the house. She had stopped attending the weekly Caring Together group some months prior to the interview: the size of the group was too much for her. She continued to use the bus into town several days a week and had just been introduced to a small neighbourhood group established by Caring Together – four people in neighbouring houses meeting locally, all of whom were in a similar situation to her, but also known to each other.

Mrs Coulter's (85) experience illustrates both the significant impact of loss and acute illness on the lifestyle she had constructed, and her struggle to sustain involvement in the things that were important to her sense of well-being. Suffering from chronic ill health for many years, she had an acute hospital admission some months prior to being interviewed, which turned into a lengthy episode when she contracted shingles. 'I haven't been right since then – lost my confidence and I can't do lots of the things I used to do.' Around the same time her daughter became seriously ill and although she was recovering, it had adversely impacted on her life in two important ways: she could not depend on her daughter 'to come and do for me like she used to'; and her weekly outing to her daughter's home had been disrupted, with the result that 'I've felt very helpless lately'. She had felt too unwell to continue with the weekly exercise group at Caring Together and to attend the day centre. Most days were organised around domestic routines interspersing jobs with a rest. At interview, Mrs Coulter described herself as 'climbing again' and had resumed attendance at the day centre – 'I'm a sociable person – better among company' – and going out with a friend on a shopping trip. She had been helped in this by a volunteer from Caring Together (Mrs Redding) who visited weekly for company – 'I get her to take me out for a walk to build up my confidence'. Like Mrs Evans, Mrs Coulter also described a life defined by poverty.

I haven't had a well-off life but I've always been able to hold my head up and that's how I want it ... I'm hoping to get better ... and as soon as I can I want to go back to the exercise group.

Lifestyle change

There were three men whose onset of ill health and/or disability had been precipitated by heavy alcohol use, leading to a dramatic change of lifestyle away from pubs and drinking mates. Their restrictions, therefore, were both social and physical. Mr Ryman (58) referred to the 'dreariness of his life' and spent a lot of time in his bed during the day. Mr Andrews (83) and Mr Richards (78) both emphasised how lonely they were – a loneliness that had its roots in their previous life histories and was not only consequent upon ageing. Mr Richards, for example, had spent most of his adult life drifting from one lodging to another. Divorced for many years, he had only intermittent contact with a sister. Ill health had forced him to reduce his drinking. His 'solitary life' had been assuaged somewhat through his pleasure in the relationship he had developed with a young couple in the locality. Even so:

> I sit here many a night on my own. I'm lonely until the weekend, when I have company *[he meets his young friends at the social club]* ... then I think to myself, 'what am I grumbling about. I've got a roof over my head. I've got a bed to lie on. I've got plenty of food in. What more do I want?'

Social isolation

There were a couple of 'younger old' women whose narrow worlds reflected as much their limited social networks as their experience of some ill health and mobility problems. Like those men who had experienced a lifestyle change and described themselves as lonely, Miss Madden's (79) restriction to the neighbourhood appeared to reflect less her ill health and disability (though she rated her health as poor) and more her social isolation: 'I have nowhere to go because I have no one to go with'. She described a solitary life: long days stretching out with little of interest to fill them – 'I take a walk around the park most days; do a bit of dusting, cleaning, cooking and washing up'. Living in a sheltered housing complex for ten years, she knew people to salute, but 'I have no friends'. Her only regular outing was (atypically) a weekly trip with her social worker into town to do the shopping.

Life on a narrow stage: restricted to the home

There were 15 older people, including two couples, who rarely ventured independently beyond their own homes. (See Appendix, Table A15 for a profile.) More than half of them were 85 years and older. Generally, the factors leading to their being restricted were similar to the previous group, although they differed in their level of severity.

There were a number of people who had experienced a gradual onset of disability as they proceeded into advanced old age. They were now at the point where physical impairments, such as loss of sight and poor mobility, meant they felt unable to get out alone. For some of them, this meant that they rarely left the confines of their own homes. Miss Coghill (95 years old) had recently given up her one regular outing – to the day centre: the effort required was not warranted by her time there.

> I used to go to the day centre but I was so long on the bus – although the centre was only up the road – that I gave it up.

She kept up daily regular contact with friends by telephone and the home care worker who came daily brought her news of friends that the worker also visited.

Mr and Mrs Murray, 90 and 87 years respectively, spent most days at home.

Mrs Murray: I can't walk and he won't go without me and I won't go without him.

Mr Murray: I'm a bit dodgy walking and my eyesight's affected – I can't see where I'm going.

Social contact had narrowed down to immediate family living in the locality: their daughter came in every morning to help with the chores; the son-in-law came in for a chat and did odd jobs; grandchildren and great-grandchildren popped in regularly.

A number of other very old people did venture out when support and transport were provided. Mrs Healy (91) and Mrs Dobson (96), both widowed for many years, were regularly collected by family members for trips out by car; likewise Mrs Nuttall (80), who, although a little younger than the others, was similar to them in that onset of disability was gradual as a result of severe arthritis. Miss Marsh (95) continued to attend a different day centre on three separate weekdays, each offering company and different kinds of activities to engage her interest: the day centre with others of her contemporaries; the club for those with a visual disability that had younger people as well; and the centre for those with a physical disability that she had attended for many years and where she had friends of long standing. On the days she was at home, friends from the locality came to visit.

For these older people, whose restriction had come on gradually, the process of adjustment evolved over time. For others, the factors precipitating a shift to 'life on a narrow stage' were a complex mix of social, psychological and physical difficulties. Mr Perring (85) had viewed himself as physically active until the onset of ill health, although his social activity and social contacts had considerably narrowed over the previous 15 years as he cared for his disabled wife. Whilst her death four years earlier had opened up possibilities for reawakening old friendships, they had not survived his confinement to the home. Ill health accompanied by pain, decreased mobility and symptoms that inspired fear and lack of confidence ('giddy spells', poor balance) had made him reluctant to leave the house:

> I've been very ill these last two years, no end of trouble … stomach … heart … I'm under about a dozen different specialists at the hospital … I'm in the house all the time now. I don't go out because these vertigo attacks come on very suddenly and if I fell outside I'd fall on concrete and I'd injure myself; whereas if I fall over in here, I've something to get hold of … I don't trust myself going out any more … the one or two friends I had picked up with, they just write now, they don't come.

For Mr Brown similarly, it was not simply his inability to get out independently that restricted him to the home but a combination of mobility problems, loss of confidence and unwillingness to be seen as disabled.

> I can't go out … I have difficulty getting into and out of a car. I don't trust myself to walk too far because I get tired very quickly … I don't have pain … it is difficulty in getting up.

Although Mr and Mrs Winston, an African-Caribbean couple, had disabilities for some years (blindness and problems with mobility) which limited how far they could get out, it was

Mrs Winston's recent illness that had pushed them over the boundary into the restricted group. This had also narrowed their social environment in that, apart from family, they no longer saw friends and acquaintances that they mostly knew from their local church. Mrs Winston did, however, go to a day centre at the hospice once a week.

> Because she can't go and my arms are not strong enough to hold her she doesn't go out – we just share life together. We read in the days ... we listen to Christian tapes.

Mrs Nunn's (89) experience of restriction was very different to that of the others considered above. Her ill health and immobility in old age were part of an ongoing pattern over the life course. She described a life dominated by physical and mental health problems: previously episodic and uneven, there was now a steady deterioration as new problems in old age such as arthritis and osteoporosis were superimposed upon long-standing chronic conditions. Her narrative was punctuated by stories of loss: of health, of a job that she took pride in, the death of her spouse and the sudden death of her only son 12 years ago. The continued salience of this loss was evident in the vividness and detail of her description of the events surrounding his death. Mrs Nunn had little contact with her remaining family, apart from Christmas cards, and although a member of Caring Together (to whom she turned for advice and assistance) she did not take part in any of the social activities. Within the sheltered complex 'nobody bobs in the flats, we don't visit each other's flats'. She did, however, spend a couple of hours with a number of other residents in the lounge of an afternoon, discussing events of the day.

Whilst this restricted group comprised more of the very old people in the study, there were also a number of younger people who had experienced an abrupt and sudden alteration of lifestyle as a result of an accident or serious and debilitating illness. Mr Fleming (61) was still working when he suffered a heart attack followed by a stroke that left him wheelchair bound. The loss of everything that had structured his life (job, hobby (walking), going to football) had 'broken my heart'. The fact that he felt unable to get out independently was an expression of the discontinuity between his identity in the past and in the present.

Experiencing restriction as a couple

In exploring 'restriction' within couples, three broad patterns emerged. First, there were those for whom the problems were mutually reinforcing but who were supportive of each other. Mrs and Mr Winston described it thus:

Mrs Winston: I can't do nothing much for myself because I can't see – I'm blind … I have cancer.

Mr Winston: She can't go out alone … I can't help her … so we don't do walking outside.

For others, differences existed in respect of their perceptions of, and mode of dealing with, restrictions. Mrs Nuttall bemoaned her husband's failure to recognise her disability and that he seemed to expect that she would look after him (although it emerged subsequently that he was suffering from dementia):

Before I was disabled it was different but now I can't get out by myself … my husband and I used to take trips out … we'd go up to the Dales, have a walk around … and we used to do quite a lot of that … and he would be better now if I could do this. I come to realise that he doesn't accept there is anything wrong with me. He sits in his chair all day long and he doesn't help in any sense at all and it can be irritating where he's bodily fit and I'm not ... While he can see me about, he's been looked after and he knows he doesn't have to look after himself ... It gets harder and you get stumped.

Similarly, Mrs Brown was frustrated at her husband for 'giving in' to his disability: his method of coping was perceived not only as a cost to her independence, it meant that he was losing out on the opportunities available.

Mr Brown: I've reached three score years and ten and I'm very comfortable ... God has been good.

Mrs Brown: That's because he's looked after ... Now you see disabled people going out, enjoying themselves ... They used to sit in a corner and do nothing but now they are living normal lives.

The third pattern is illustrated by the experience of Mr and Mrs Carrington. Mr Carrington (78) was severely disabled as a result of a series of strokes. Mrs Carrington (80) was being supported by an extensive package of formal care that she described as 'hospital at home' – two carers three times a day and some hours' respite a month. Her major preoccupation, however, was not only help with caring tasks but to continue to involve her husband in both 'ordinary' activities and regular social events they had enjoyed doing together in the past and which were still important to them. Thus, once a week they went dancing – Mr Carrington to watch and see old friends and acquaintances – and on Saturday mornings, they went into town – he to the barber's, she to the hairdresser. Sustaining this social life provoked major and ongoing hassles with obstacles to be overcome at every step to secure appropriate transport. He could no longer get into a car or a taxi. It was difficult to get Dial-a-Ride transport to coincide with the dance group: if they got there on time, they would often have to leave early or very late. Mrs Carrington was passionate in her efforts to get services to understand the importance of preserving the quality of her husband's life, but it was an uphill struggle.

Life on a narrow stage: securing well-being

Generally, whilst physical restrictions had placed limits on people's social activity, their sense of well-being was sustained by the degree to which they continued to do things that were pleasurable to them, their 'social world' came to them and/or they were able to get out with the support of family and friends.

Mrs Nuttall described a 'good life' that embraced an 'outing' once a week with one or other of her daughters when they dressed up and went somewhere special – a trip in the car, lunch, visiting relatives – and a daily routine – cooking, baking, doing bits about the house, a pop-in visit from her son every evening with the newspaper – that was punctuated by what she termed her 'distractions' – her friend's social call, a visit from her hairdresser, a visit from her sister. Mrs Dobson's social life had increasingly narrowed down to her immediate family living locally. She no longer went to coffee mornings in her sheltered housing complex 'because I can't hear so well and I want to be able to hear properly what is being said'. Her family collected her a couple of times a week and took her to their house. She described herself as having always helped others. Now, although her son and daughter-in-law helped with laundry and shopping, when she went to them, 'I help out with the ironing and drying up … I like to help out. I can't sit idle. That's what keeps me going'. She described herself as content: 'I think I'll end my days beautiful if it goes on like this'. Mrs Healy's restriction to the home was more recent and contrasted with her life of active involvement in church and community activities. Ordinary things that had been previously taken for granted loomed large whilst apparently simple activities were now sources of pleasure:

> I would like to go out of the door and go for a little walk around … I just miss going to the shops and picking my own things. I just manage. Now and again I get up and have a walk around with my wheeler and look out the window … I can see people I know going by … as long as I can still see and hear … and read my books and do my puzzles.

Indeed a common theme in the narratives of the very old – those in their tenth decade – was the pleasure of being alive and being able to enjoy each day:

> I see a bit of sunshine in a morning and I thank God for making me so bright and cheerful.

For these very old people, simple pleasures, the company of family and friends and the sense of contentment from a life well lived assumed more importance than new experiences:

> I've done it all and I'm content now.

> I've had my life. I've got a lot to be thankful for.

> I've had a happy life.

> Being able to move about a bit and to see and hear – I'm content.

Whilst they may not have been 'active' in the sense of those who were 'out and about', they were engaged – being part of networks of social relationships.

Generally, however, where there was an absence of, or minimal, social contact or people perceived that there was little in their lives that gave them pleasure, well-being was compromised for this group. Mrs Nunn's description of her life illustrates this in the starkest terms:

> In about ten days, I'll be 89 – terrible isn't it … I know there is nothing to look forward to … It's not worth the bother to go out and meet people … I don't want to go to a day centre … they're not my line … I don't want to paint flowers, I don't want to roll little balls into a hole, I don't even want to play bingo … I don't want to sing songs … I'm not a party person at all … The one thing I do … in the afternoon there's about four of us go downstairs most afternoons and sit and chat in the lounge. We talk about all sorts of things, gossip – I don't mean about people … but what's going on in the world … Strangers come in and say 'Haven't you got a television' … but we can do that in our own place.

For some of the others, loss or contraction of social networks had been partially compensated for by the introduction of a volunteer befriender. Mr Perring described the pleasure he derived from this weekly visit. That and 'keeping my brain active … doing puzzles and reading … are what keep me going'.

Managing day-to-day life: general themes

We now turn to consider some general themes that emerged across all of the interviews in terms of managing day-to-day life over the ageing process:

- managing time

- dealing with 'daily hassles'

- negotiating the physical environment.

Managing time

Across all of the interviews – from those who spent most of their time 'out and about' to those who were restricted to home and neighbourhood – lives were structured in patterns that had a daily and weekly rhythm.

For those older people who were active in leisure and community activities, there was not enough time to do everything.

> When you think what you do now, you wonder how you had time to work.

> They say when you retire you need eight days in the week.

> My family say they have to make an appointment to see me.

> I get messages left on the answer machine from my family, 'you're never in when I need you'.

> I've done a lot more than I ever thought was possible – the only time I'm in is when I do my chores.

An important difference, however, between the 'busyness' currently and that when they worked was that now they were doing things they enjoyed doing.

At the other end of the age spectrum, those in advanced old age spoke about organising their days 'pottering around doing little things'. For them, 'pottering about' reflected the fact that the tasks of day-to-day life took longer: 'I do a little bit, and then I rest'. Low energy levels, moreover, meant that they took little naps during the day. Mrs Dobson confessed that: 'sometimes in the afternoon, I fall off to sleep. Isn't that awful!'

Making choices and prioritising

In managing their lives, interviewees constantly referred to making choices and assessing priorities across all of the interviews. This had a different meaning for people who spent their lives 'out and about' and those restricted by ill health and disability. It was notable, for example, that doing the chores assumed less importance for older people who were out and about. In part it was because they felt they had better things to do with their time; in part it reflected the fact that life was spent mostly outside the home. This is illustrated graphically in the following excerpt from one of the focus groups:

Q: Are there things you give up now?

Miss Jackman: I just give up housework, me.

Mrs Mattocks: I do.

Mrs Melville: I don't do the same housework as I did. I don't change curtains or clean windows as often.

Mrs Flowers: We got one of those squeegee things *[lots of laughter as Mrs Flowers explains how she tried to use it]*.

Mrs Mattocks: I use the hosepipe.

Mrs Melville: I pray for rain.

Q: Does it worry you about the housework?

Everybody: No – unless anyone is coming and then it's a quick hoover around.

Mrs Melville: You don't ask friends home do you? I don't.

Mrs Mattocks: My mum used to say 'more people pass by than come in'.

For people who were restricted to the home, not only was the physical state of their environment more significant to them, they were also more conscious of the gap between the standards to which they aspired and their limitations. Having a clean home was central to their sense of well-being.

Dealing with daily hassles

A major source of stress for many older people were what have been termed 'daily hassles', the 'irritating, frustrating, distressing demands and troubled relationships that plague us day in and day out' (Lazarus and DeLongis, 1983, p. 247). Chronic sources of stress, for example in long-term illness such as heart disease or arthritis, more prevalent among older people, must be lived with and managed rather than resolved.

We identified different types of 'daily hassles' that were a major source of stress for people in the study. These included: the constant reminders of the death of a spouse or close friend when faced with having to deal with the tasks which that person had previously undertaken; the myriad of little things that they could either not do, or found difficulty in doing, because of increasing disabilities – unscrewing jars, changing light bulbs, sweeping leaves from the gutters, putting up and taking down curtains, and cleaning windows; frustration with a spouse on account of the way they responded to a disability or the constant struggle to do some things together as a couple where one of them was disabled; the continuous challenge of having to resolve problems that were previously taken for granted – negotiating hilly and/or uneven terrain and being able to sit down whilst out shopping; the worry of maintaining the fabric and decoration of their homes. The frustrations generated by these daily hassles were twofold: that in the absence of family, friends or neighbours, there was no obvious source of help with them; and that they foreshadowed an escalation of dependence.

> I've always had to look after myself, think for myself and do things for myself. And now I get irritated because little things I could do for myself, I can't do. I can't have the kitchen window open. To shut it, I can't fasten it they are so stiff, so I have to leave it shut.

> My hallway's a mess. It was stripped ages ago, ready to decorate and now it's waiting to be done. It is sitting there thinking about it. It gets on top of me.

> Life's completely changed, I can't go out unless someone takes me … So I'm in all the time in that grotty little flat. You know, looking at what's around. And you know you can't get up to do the curtains or the decorating.

Asked if anything made life difficult for them as they became older, Mr and Mrs Murray responded:

> Not being able to do things that we used to do. We used to do all our own decorating and we can't do that now. We used to do the garden which we can't do. I mean he used to grow tomatoes and everything in the garden but we can't now.

In dealing with the 'daily hassles', several important issues arise. First, there is a need to focus on how people develop strategies for managing ongoing sources of stress such as chronic illness and the vicissitudes of ageing and how these might be built upon. Second, it is evident that people have differential access to resources to deal with them. Having sufficient income to pay someone to clean or decorate the house, for example, means that one does not have to suffer the frustration of being unable to do it oneself. Third, there is the question of how services might provide appropriate assistance to help people manage the 'daily hassles', whilst also taking into account their differential access to resources.

Negotiating the physical environment

While dealing with the daily hassles may be seen as one of the challenges in coping with the micro-environment through the ageing process, ways of negotiating the external environment, especially for those with lower levels of mobility and energy, was a feature of both the interviews and the focus groups. Access to premises which had steps, availability of somewhere to sit down and rest, and suitable forms of transport all exercised the minds of people before they ventured from their homes.

Getting out and about

Today I walked to the market but there are some seats and I have a little rest, walk down toward the market, sit down again and then go through the market and that's it. Shopping, get the bus and come home. It really is a marvellous place to help us to manage ourselves. But if there are no seats and you have to walk straight, I wouldn't be able to.

There are times when I get in the shopping centre and there is nowhere to sit down and I say I am not going to cry. You think how much further have I to go before I can see the end of that seat. It's so frustrating when you get there and you think I should not be like this.

A recurring theme from the interviews was the obstacles and challenges posed for older people in going about their daily lives by the physical features of the places in which they lived. The nature of the terrain in Woodhouse, in particular, is difficult for older people to negotiate. From the central thoroughfare of Woodhouse Street, steep hills of terraces, flats and small estates radiate upwards and outwards. To move outside one's door in any direction involves climbing a hill. What was taken for granted in youth by Mrs Daltry was an ever-present reality in old age.

I was only a spring chicken when we came here but as you get older you find the footpaths, the steps, and the hill … it's quite a climb. We can't get up the hill.

Moreover, since very few older people in this area owned a car and were reliant on public transport, their difficulties were compounded by the bus routes in operation. There was not a single bus that went all the way from the city centre at the bottom of the hill to the Ridge at the top: all stopped halfway. Given the value placed by them on getting out and about and the social significance of the trip to the shops, this was a particularly salient issue for older people.

> I get off the bus *[at the end – midway]* and walk up the
> hill and if you've got some shopping, it's a really big hill
> to climb, especially for old people. L *[neighbour]* couldn't
> do it.

Indeed, in a very real sense, for older people in this area who
were reliant on public transport, the bus route dictated where
they went. Thus, whilst Age Concern had its centre a short walk
up the hill from Woodhouse, there was very little use of its facilities
by local people: it was mainly used by those travelling in from
the outer suburbs on a direct bus route. Although the bus station
was located on the other side of the city, people tended to use
the bus for day trips, since they could get a direct bus to the bus
station; the train station, though geographically closer, involved a
long walk, or several buses. Similarly, a number of those
interviewed did their shopping at a small township several miles
away, because the local bus service went there.

Whilst a number of people in the study used the Access bus,
trips were rationed and choices had to be made, as Mrs Nyman
explained:

> I'm so thankful to have the Access bus once a week …
> When I asked for an Access bus, the man who sent me
> the form said I was not really supposed to have so many.
> So I asked 'how many is too many, could I have a second
> one for the church' and he said 'was it a priority'. Well,
> my priority really is the Playhouse so he said I should
> just ask for that … So I only get the one.

In Hartlepool, the RRN had achieved some success in
campaigning for a better physical environment for older people:
seats and shelters at bus stops and seats in the main shopping
centre.

Summary

In exploring the day-to-day lives of older people, what is revealed is a picture of diversity, continuity and change. Whilst there is no single lifestyle that encapsulates 'successful' ageing, what did emerge were several themes or factors that appeared necessary to sustain people's sense of well-being:

- having the capacity and opportunity to be involved in different types of social, leisure and stimulating activities that connected them to people and places with whom they shared interests and experiences

- a continued enjoyment of mutually supportive, intimate and companionable relationships

- the ability to do things that brought pleasure and meaning.

Among those 'out and about 'older people, there were some whose need for sociability and stimulation was met primarily within spousal and family relationships. For others, shared activities and interests engaged them in multiple networks both within and outside their neighbourhoods. People did indeed develop new, intimate and companionable relationships in old age, which in turn stimulated interest in social, educational, community and leisure activities. Whilst understanding, empathy and shared interests were critical in the formation of these relationships, of significance as well was that people had access to a range of forums and opportunities to meet people.

Also revealed was an enormous commitment to, and capacity for, involvement in community and other groups, reflecting an outward and 'other-centred' approach to life. Whilst for some older people, this was an extension of a lifelong interest in action for change and improvement, for others, particularly women, it was their 'liberation' from the routines of managing home and family that provided the impetus for them to get involved in community and other groups. The capacity and interest revealed among those working for the community, moreover, demonstrate both the breadth and depth of experience of older people as a force for change and the potential resource that can be built upon within localities to support and sustain 'healthy' communities.

In the main, people who for various reasons were restricted to the home or to the immediate locality struggled to continue doing things that they found pleasurable and meaningful. Adjustment to their changing situation might involve them in difficult decisions and having to choose between competing priorities. Most problematic, however, was the fact that often it was a case of selecting the least negative option because of the way services were rationed or delivered.

Even so, restriction to the home or immediate neighbourhood did not in itself mean that people were socially isolated. The key factor was whether people's social worlds came to them or they were enabled to get out and about. For some of those in advanced old age, however, a contraction of their spatial world on account of ill health, disability and declining vigour might also be accompanied by a narrowing down of their social worlds to immediate family.

Differential access to resources made a difference to people's life quality in the face of restrictions. Having a car, for example, or having enough money to afford a taxi, meant that one could get out and about despite problems with mobility. At the same time, living within a poor physical environment with inadequate local services such as shops and buses could exacerbate the problems posed by ill health and disability.

It was notable that the locality focus of Caring Together played a critical role in sustaining people's social worlds in the face of restriction: through its array of leisure and social groups of different sizes, and varied levels of 'activism', and through creative endeavours that sought to tailor solutions to people's specific interests and needs. But for more active older people as well, Caring Together was an important part of their everyday lives. The range of activities on offer was a source of enjoyment and stimulation, provided opportunities for renewing and making new friends and acquaintances, offered a framework for 'neighbourly' action and reciprocal support, and generated a sense of belonging to a 'community', to which they were valued contributors. In Hartlepool, on the other hand, the RRN provided an important forum for some older people to engage in social action towards making a better life for themselves and their peers.

6 SOCIAL RELATIONSHIPS AND SOCIAL SUPPORT

The existence of relationships that link people together and meet a wide range of needs, physical, social, intellectual and emotional, is a fundamental feature of all social life. The importance to older people of maintaining a sense of their own self-identity and purpose has been demonstrated in previous chapters. Likewise, older people's sociability and engagement were central to their conception of well-being. As older people reflected on what they valued in life, they spoke frequently about the importance of having a 'good' family, 'good' friend or 'good' neighbour.

In this chapter, we look at older people within a landscape peopled by families, friends, neighbours and interest groups. First, we consider the different kinds of social networks of older people within our two localities. Second, we examine social relationships and social support within these networks and the factors that contributed to variation over the ageing process.

Older people's social networks

Older people living alone dominated in our sample (65 per cent overall). Just under one-third lived with a spouse; five people lived with unmarried sons who had continued to live in the family home and one Asian elder lived with his wife and teenage child. Just under one-fifth of people had never married.

There were small numbers in both Hartlepool and Leeds of traditional, close-knit extended families where adult children lived in the same street and grandchildren, brothers and sisters, nieces and nephews, lived close by. There were other older people whose adult children had their own households in the local area. For the majority, however, children lived further away from older parents, in other parts of the town and city and outside the area, reflecting migration for education and work.

Although the family remained the core of most people's social networks, there was a small group of people who had no close family ties.

Beyond the family, social networks comprised friends, neighbours, acquaintances and people with common interests. Most of those with close family nearby

Mutual support from family and friends

also had wide-ranging ties with friends and neighbours. Many of those who had never married, women in particular, had extensive networks of friends. Several also had considerable contact with, and support from, nieces and nephews. In some instances this related to people bringing up nieces and nephews as their own children in earlier days. For some there was an intimate relationship with a special friend that was as significant to them as that of a partner or spouse. A very small number of people were extremely isolated – with neither regular contact with family nor close relationships with friends.

In the following discussion, we consider the nature and types of support available within social networks, the factors that contributed to variation and the significance of locality in shaping people's access to and availability of support.

Social relationships and support

A wide range of personal needs (emotional, social, physical and practical) was addressed within different relationship ties. A clear picture emerged from the interviews of two often parallel networks of older people, one based on family and the other on friends and neighbours. These were seen as operating in different ways, although in practice the differences were not so clear-cut.

> Well I think you've got two social networks, you've got those, your own family, which of course is natural but it is very important I think to have a social network of people who are not your family, people who are your contemporaries, people who you can relate to. You don't relate to your children in the same way as you relate to your contemporaries.

We now examine in more detail the significance of the different types of relationships within which people were enmeshed.

Family

In the locally based extended-family networks, where people lived close to their own children, grandchildren and siblings, there was a strong articulation of the importance of the family unit.

> Mixing with people, we always mixed with people. We were both from a close family. I have three sisters now and a brother – we're like a unit, if anybody wants anything we are there but we always have time for other people. I mean my younger sister she looks after the mother-in-law who is 95 and lives on her own. I went to see her the other day because they [sister and family] were on holiday, so I had to fit her in. Then I rang my other sister's daughter because she is expecting a baby and her husband is in America.

The family gravitated towards active older people within these networks: their homes were the centre for family gatherings at Christmas or for Sunday dinner. For example, Mrs Hyde described how her children and grandchildren popped in for meals after work.

> Like today ... my daughter will come in from work and she'll say 'Oh I don't have to cook'. She comes up here, you see. And they'll come home from school. The other daughter brings the little ones home from school. They're fed before they go home. It's like a cafeteria. I wouldn't be without them.

Flow of support

The reciprocal nature of family relationships was evident in the interviews. Not only did older people attach considerable value to reciprocity but their accounts of their relationships with family emphasised the two-way flow of support. This is illustrated in the following from Mrs Kennedy (83):

> My son comes over and he does do quite a lot for me, when it is a job I can't do for myself, but if it is anything I can do myself, he says 'get on with it'. I think if I'm doing something it's better for my arthritis and for my body, better for myself ... He won't do the garden, he hates gardening. So I go over and cut his lawn. He works hard, he's at the steelworks and he's got a family.

Where people suffered ill health or were disabled, the emphasis was on doing as much as possible for themselves. Here too, they sought to maintain some reciprocity in the relationship, even where adult children and grandchildren were providing regular, practical help, as we saw in Chapter 4.

For a number of those in advanced old age, people spoke of a lower level of energy affecting social engagement and relationships with close family were prioritised over other types of relationships. Mrs Dobson (96), who had been very sociable in her younger life, spoke about not being bothered about going to the day room to socialise with other residents in the sheltered housing complex. This was due partly to low energy and partly to deafness, which made socialisation hard work. However, she left her door open so that people could 'bob' in for a chat. What was most important to her was her involvement in and relationships with immediate family to whom she still provided regular assistance (ironing and washing up). Mr and Mrs Murray, who were similarly restricted to their home, had little contact with others beyond their immediate family. They relied heavily on their daughter and grandchildren for emotional, social and practical support. Even so, Mrs Murray still cooked a special hotpot for her daughter on the day when she was making one.

> To tell you the truth, now we are buying those meals from *[the supermarket]* – we are practically living on them. But he keeps on that he wants a meat and potato pie. And if I make a casserole tomorrow, I make one for me and one for our Jane, because she works on Saturdays and she can't make a proper meal.

For people who were making the transition to becoming more dependent, negotiating mutually acceptable help could be fraught with frustration and difficulties. For example, Mrs Varley was annoyed that her son had replaced all the electrical plugs at a higher level to stop her from having to bend down.

Mrs Varley: Look what my son has done at the weekend. He makes me feel 90. He's put all the plugs on there.

Q: Is that so it is easier for you?

Mrs Varley:	I can manage them. They were only just on the floor.
Q:	But has he done it to make life easier?
Mrs Varley:	I'd appreciate it more if he did his bedroom …
Q:	Ah bless him, he tried didn't he.
Mrs Varley:	Yes but he doesn't try for the things that I want trying.

It was evident that some older people had strong views about what help was appropriate for their families to provide. Mrs Nuttall went on regular social outings with her daughters, but would not ask them to do certain chores.

> My kitchen drain smells terrible because I used to go out every Friday morning and take a bucket of hot water, a small brush, and scrub down that grate and keep it clean and tidy. I can't do it now. I'm damn sure that when my children come dressed up I'm not going to ask them to clean the grate out. I'm not going to ask them.

Mrs Alcock had been distressed when she was assessed for help post-discharge from hospital to be told by the social worker that she could not have home care help for her cleaning and shopping because she had a supportive family.

Acknowledging limits, boundaries and traditional roles

Distance affected the extent to which support could be offered, though several people spoke of having their grandchildren to stay during the holidays or of doing jobs for the children when they went to visit them. Telephone contact on a regular basis was an important feature of more distant family networks.

Some older people noted the effect of distance on the nature of relationships. Most said that their children had their own lives to lead and laid much emphasis on not wanting to hold them back. However, at one of the focus groups there was discussion about the qualitative impact of distance, even where practical help and support were offered.

> And the children have moved away and the link isn't strong enough – they have their own lives to lead. I feel I'm very much on the fringe somehow. I would like a special place but there isn't the opportunity to do this.

> That's exactly how I feel with my family having gone away. The only time I'm needed is when they want a babysitter.

Proximity alone was not the only determining factor in how often older people saw their families. Relationship difficulties and tensions between family members affected contact for some. A more frequent issue was the other commitments of adult children to work, their families and their own health problems. This affected both how often they saw each other and what help the older people felt they could ask of their children.

> You get practical problems that you need to resolve. I am fortunate. As I say I've got a good family and while they are all tied up working and whatever, you know that they are there. I feel rather sorry for my elder daughter because she manages a residential home and she's dealing with older people all day, all the time. When we are out on Tuesday, she's pushing my wheelchair. I said to her 'It's like a busman's holiday'. She said 'Mum, it's different when it's you'. It is different but it is hard.

My sons have taken me out but not lately. They both have busy jobs. They are working night and day actually during the year. Oh it's hard work and weekends as well.

Where parents lived with their adult children (all sons in this study), in the main this was because they had never left home. The older women, for the most part, maintained their motherly role in preparing meals and doing the housework for their sons, who reciprocated by helping with heavier work such as decorating or escorting them if they went out at night. Mr Andrews, speaking about his mother with whom he had lived all his life, said that she had continued to look after him until her death. He had not had anything to do in the home and consequently found it difficult to cope with basic housework and cooking when she died. A mutually dependent household of father and disabled son provided support for each other. The son was very physically disabled but controlled the running of the household and drove his car to the supermarket. His 92-year-old father, who was becoming confused, was taken round by the supermarket staff to do the shopping. He also prepared the meals in the home.

Grandchildren

Grandchildren were an obvious source of pride, affection and interest to many of the older people; houses were full of photographs of younger generations. They talked warmly about their grandchildren's achievements.

Where people lived locally to their grandchildren, there were often close and valued relationships. The care offered by active grandparents for grandchildren has been noted above. As older people were becoming frailer, some grandchildren living nearby were active in giving support, both practical and emotional.

Mrs Lightfoot's grandson was the mainstay of support when her husband was terminally ill in hospital.

Mrs Lightfoot: Oh that was awful, if it hadn't been for my grandson Colin and his wife. He had a car and he could come for me at lunchtime and take me and we would go back at night. It was awful.

Q: It sounds as if you have a lot of support from your grandchildren.

Mrs Lightfoot: No I don't actually. There is only the one – Colin my eldest grandson. The other two live a life of their own – they do cuddle and love me when they come but that's it. I get a cuddle and a kiss but there is a long distance between visits. Colin comes regularly and brings his son.

Older people who did not see their grandchildren often regretted the social changes which had led to a greater physical distance between grandparent and grandchild. Mrs Bates reflected:

When my youngest son was growing up, my mother lived near and we used to see a lot of her. She used to come to me for the day until it got that she came to me altogether. But the link between him and his grandmother was such that at the time I used to think how wonderful it was and wish that if I lived long enough I would have such a relationship.

Mrs Nunn was indignant that her grandson had not explained to her what he meant when he said simply that he had a job in software.

If they told me, explained to me, I'd know about these things. I can understand but they don't tell me because they think I'm too old.

From many older people, there were concerns for their grandchildren stemming from an awareness of changed social values. There was discussion in one focus group about grandchildren and great-grandchildren as reminders to them of their old age.

For those who did not have children or grandchildren, nieces, nephews, grand-nieces and grand-nephews often substituted for the emotional and practical support that closer relatives tended to provide. Miss Marsh's grand-niece came weekly with her son to do a big clean; and Miss Marsh reciprocated by entertaining her great-grand-nephew and preparing lunch for everyone. Mrs Myerscroft, who had no children of her own, was visited a couple of times a week by her niece on her way home from work. Miss Mills was in regular contact with her nephew in America.

Siblings

For many older people siblings were an important part of their lives. For example, Mrs Bennett spoke of her childhood, when she had been a 'sickly child'. Her sister had always looked after her and defended her when necessary at school. In older age, she still referred to the help that her sister would offer and turned to her for help in accessing services or sorting out practicalities. Social visits and telephone contact with sisters and brothers were a regular, valued part of the weekly pattern of life. Some women talked about keeping a motherly eye on their brothers, who lived alone. Mr Hutton explained, after answering the phone during the interview:

> That was my sister. She's always concerned. My mother passed away when I was a year old and she brought me up but she is like a mother to me. She lives in Wakefield but she keeps in contact with me every day to see everything is all right – she's older than me.

Mrs Mason, a lady who was too immobile to leave her home independently, spoke of her responsibility to her sister.

Mrs Mason: I have a sister in Gosport Lane, she's got Alzheimer's. I have to look after her.

Q: How do you get out?

Mrs Mason: My son takes me in the car and I go and have a little chat with her but at the moment she does not know anybody. She has two daughters but they don't come, so she comes on to me.

Friends

Significance of friendships

Although family – including siblings, grandchildren, nieces and nephews – were a primary source of comfort and support, it is evident from previous chapters that friends were the mainstay of most people's day-to-day lives: sharing experiences, pleasure and pain, providing companionship in social activities and supporting people through life changes, such as bereavement. In this respect, our findings differ from those of Phillipson *et al.* (2001), who suggested that friends played a more significant role in middle-class

"Good friends are important"

than in working-class networks among the older people they studied.

Within the working-class neighbourhoods of Woodhouse and Little London as well as in the more socially mixed town of Hartlepool, the importance of friends as sources of emotional and social support was a significant theme of the interviews.

People differentiated between the kinds of friendships developed in different types of activities and the different kinds of support they derived from them. For example, Mr Edmonds had engaged in an extensive range of activities since his early widowhood and retirement, through which he had cultivated different kinds of relationships. He distinguished between his close friendships developed at the gym where he shared experiences and enjoyed a laugh and more intermittent social contacts in interest and community groups that were a source of conversation and stimulation. Miss Openshaw spoke of younger friends, who came to offer practical help when she was ill, of neighbours who took her shopping and of good friends who shared her interests in alternative therapy and healing, while also enjoying a different type of engagement within the Retired Resource Network.

It was evident that most people had some friends on whom they could rely for practical help, for example if they were ill or had experienced a crisis or just to look after their pets when they went away. Mrs Mitchell talked with gratitude of all the help she had received recently since she had become ill: for her daily home care visits, for the support of her daughter and grandson, for the emotional support provided by her friends from church and the practical and emotional help given by her friend and neighbour who visited every night, sat with her and helped her to bed. Miss Marsh, who was restricted to her home other than attendance at day centres, had an extensive network of friends, neighbours and family. Four of her friends from the local area did her shopping and helped with her pensions and bills. A close neighbour helped with bathing and laundry. Similar patterns of support could be observed for a few other older people, well integrated into their locality. There was significant support by friends in small practical tasks such as shopping. Mrs Morris, who had converted to Islam, emphasised the reciprocal nature of exchange over time:

> There's also a friend, she used to live on the same street with her children. When I used to come in from work, I would ask them about school and how they got on, because sometimes she was at work. I used to get little books and a pen for them and if she was going shopping on Saturday morning, I'm going back years, she would always leave them with me. I'd sit down and help them with whatever I could help them with. So now if I want anything from the shops she gets it for me ... goes especially to get me halal meat – I'm a Muslim – and sometimes vegetables and stuff like that, which is nice and I'm grateful.

In previous chapters, we considered some key transition points, such as retirement and bereavement, that potentially threaten size and composition of social networks. The issue, however, was not simply about loss but about the resources and opportunities that people could draw upon to develop alternative sources of support.

Where people had worked actively in retirement at developing new interests, their networks had expanded or renewed. For women, in particular, the loss of their spouse through death when they were still in good health was often the trigger for developing new interests and relationships as they moved away from a family-centred life to a wider community-based one. Mrs Kennedy spoke of different groups of friends acquired over her lifetime – some at the dancing club she attended with her husband, others relating to long-standing work with a charitable organisation. More recently she had made many friends at the local bowling club and via active involvement in the national league she had friends all over the country. Added to this widening circle, she developed a deep friendship with an old acquaintance whose husband had recently died.

> It's only a recent friendship truthfully, she lost her husband 18 months ago and until then I knew her just to say hello but nothing close. I would say to her 'Do you want a lift home' or something like that and brought her home. She said 'Alice, if you fancy going out anywhere, will you call for me because I'm awfully lonely on my own since my husband's gone'. Until then I hadn't even thought she could be lonely because she had a son and grandchildren, one of the granddaughters came to live with her so I knew she had company all the time. And since then we've got on like a house on fire together, it's amazing but we've really struck it well together. So she's a good companion to me. Before that I had companions but nothing as close as we are.

Local groups played an important role in providing a further arena for friendships to be sustained and developed. We noted in previous chapters the role played by Caring Together in renewing acquaintances and cementing friendships that had been loosened as a result of the demands of marriage, family and work. Mrs Jennings from Hartlepool told a similar story. She had bumped into a woman at a shop in town and engaged in casual conversation, remembering her as someone from childhood. As they brought each other up to date with key life events, including the recent deaths of their respective husbands, on Mrs Jennings's prompting, her childhood friend was encouraged to come along with her to the Friendship Group and the Widows Association.

The existence of community groups in localities also offered a base for those who moved into an area to forge new networks.

> I've just recently moved from Manchester. My daughter lives here in Hartlepool and she wanted me to move so I said OK I'll think about it and finally I decided that I'd move. I thought I can't be fully dependent on her so I've really got to get myself out and about and get myself into some group or whatever and get mobile, because I'd worked more or less right up to being 63 full time and I still miss that. I spoke to the lady next door and she said that she goes along to these pensioners' meetings and asked if I was interested. So she said if you want to come along, so that was it and so that was the first time I'd been when you arrived on the Monday.

Long-time residence in a locality meant that friendships were often of considerable longevity, with links into people's childhood and youth, as we noted earlier. Two women, who had been neighbours for 50 years, developed the notion of friendships coming full circle. After their husbands died they spent more of their days together and were mutually supportive of each other on a day-to-day basis.

> As you know I go with Edith, we're great friends. You see Edith came here same time as me, we moved in the same week. She came to no. 52 and I came to no. 58 and when the kids were little we used to go on holiday together and then we started going for a night out, one girlie night out. And things like that, so gradually we've done a full circle and got back to what we used to be doing.

Within Woodhouse and Little London, there was a strong network of friends that had developed through long-time involvement in church and chapel and was reinforced by locality ties. Church fellowships, which continued for most people as they became housebound, were an important source of emotional and social support. For some of the black and minority ethnic elders, cultural connectedness was also significant.

> I go to the temple most days. Today is Guru Nanak's birthday and those of us who are qualified read from the holy book for three days. I go to the nearest temple but we get invitations to other Sikh temples ... But there are not many Sikh people in this area you know. They used to live here but they have gone.

Churches could also offer intergenerational friendships which were valued.

> When I moved here, I found the church and they accepted me, they were very, very good. One of the girls is coming tomorrow. She rang me and asked if I could go. She's got the day off work and she would like to take me out somewhere. They are very good at helping me to send parcels and things home and that – it is a family ... They take me once for the weekend to the Lake District and they were asking me every year to come with us. I said, 'I don't know'. Well they are all young. If they want to do something, I'll be holding them back. One year they insisted and I went and I enjoyed it and they enjoyed my company. They are still talking about it because I could do a lot more things and I'm more flexible than they are, they were laughing and they are still mentioning it.

Eight people involved in a chapel in the centre of Woodhouse gave an insight into the functions of church networks within the locality. These offered support to members in a range of circumstances – at points of crisis or need for practical help, in caring relationships, as they became frailer and less able to attend church. Miss Jackman, for example, was confident that help would be forthcoming when needed.

> But we know at church that we have only to ring someone up and someone will be there.

Her experience during her mother's illness had reinforced this confidence.

> I've been a Methodist since I was eleven. I got a lot of comfort and help from my church. They rallied round and went to see Mum when I was away. Because I usually went to see her every day but they took it in turns to visit her so that there was never a time when no one went to see her. She couldn't speak but she could understand.

The church contacts were characterised by reciprocity. For example, when Miss Jackman spoke of help in relation to her mother, another church member added:

> But Miss Jackman used to drive a car in those days. We used to go lots of places in that car. She was so generous with lifts.

Two women who were housebound kept in touch with each other by telephone to cheer each other up.

> The main thing is having somebody to talk with. If Margaret gets fed up, she phones me and I phone her and we keep in touch that way, even if it's only to talk about what we are watching or what we are doing.

Illness and increased disability could have an adverse effect on friendship networks. Similarly, caring responsibilities also had the potential to restrict social engagement. As we noted in Chapter 5, there were a number of people interviewed who had experienced lifestyle changes that had involved them in a shift from a social life based on pubs and clubs and resulted in the loss of 'mates'. Contraction of networks was neither inevitable nor irreversible, however.

As people became restricted to their immediate locality, their networks were affected but the impact on friendships showed differentially. Mrs Myerscroft told of her loss of contact with friends from the bowling club who did not live in the area. However, she retained her local friends, based around the church, and began to attend a small group developed by Caring Together for those who were restricted by ill health. For others, like Miss Marsh and Mrs Mitchell above, friends came to them.

A number of those interviewed did not have what they described as 'friends'. Rather, in contemplating the nature of their networks, they distinguished between 'being friendly with people' and not having a friend. This phrase was used repeatedly to describe relationships at day centres or interest groups and to distinguish them from earlier close friendships which had meant a great deal to them. Mrs Sharma explained the limits of her expectations of friends in her interest circles:

Mrs Sharma: Not friends. Friendship is very difficult. I know a lot of people in a friendly way.

Q: Could you explain to me about that?

Mrs Sharma: Intimacy is very difficult, very sacrificing. People are very good with you, but when you need help, they do help in some ways but you need help in many ways.

In describing the impact of the death of her lifelong companion in Chapter 4, Miss Goodman made a similar distinction between friendships based on intimacy and those based on shared interests. With the former, there were no boundaries around what was appropriate to share or get help for: the phrase 'I was there for her and she was there for me' expressed the unconditional nature of the relationship.

Neighbours and neighbouring

Neighbours were an integral part of people's social networks in both Leeds and Hartlepool, not surprisingly given that most of the people in our study had lived in their current localities for over 20 years. Only a tiny number of those interviewed were unable to name at least one neighbour who provided them with support or for whom they provided help, although the intensity and nature of help varied.

Many people talked of exchanges of help, such as having each other's keys and keeping an eye on the house when someone was away, or help they had given at a time of crisis such as burglary, flood, illness or bereavement.

> I like giving as much as receiving. It's gracious to receive and my friends down the road, her husband grows veggies, beetroots, beans and everything and there's always too much for them and sometimes they come over and put carriers at the back door. When she wants something big, I take her shopping because they haven't a car.

> Well you see, they are mostly students but next door but one, she lost her mother a couple of years ago. Well I helped her with that.

The people in this street don't talk to each other, but my neighbour next door, they lived there when I moved in, they're Jamaican type of people and they're lovely and we don't pop in and out of each other's houses, but I know that they're there. My house flooded over a year ago and they knocked me up because of all the water coming out and helped me get all the carpets up. Now at this side I keep having different people, when I first moved in Anne lived there and she was a good neighbour and she liked to come in for a cup of coffee or have me in there, that's the kind of neighbours, not nosy. Now the lady at no. 1 has never spoken to us, she walks down there and she never even looks across the road.

A valued role adopted by neighbours was that of keeping an eye out for each other. Frequently this was described as a role assumed by men.

Mrs Myerscroft: I can't grumble about neighbours. I mean mine next door, he comes every day to see me – twice a day. If he goes out at night, he comes and tells me before he goes and he says, 'Don't you open that door. Keep it locked'.

Mrs Ismay: When I come home it is only about 10.40 p.m., my next door neighbour is still up, his lights are on and I've noticed that he must hear my door go and then I've seen his light go out and I thought I bet he's waited until he's heard me get in.

Q: Is he getting on?

Mrs Ismay: Well I don't know how old he is, he's a big tall fellow and he's not right young.

Q: But you don't have a lot to do with him I suppose, you know he's there.

Mrs Ismay: Oh yes and he' s told me if I'm not so well or I want anything fetching, he'll bring it. But I won't ask him, I've plenty in.

A number of older people extended their neighbourly role to caring about the wider environment in the area. Thus people spoke of taking responsibility for dealing with litter or of attending local council meetings to raise neighbourhood issues: some who could not get out and about spoke of contacting the council to get repairs or tree cutting done. Other people had actively collaborated in a very successful Neighbourhood Watch scheme.

Active older people frequently shopped for their neighbours, seeing this as having a value for themselves as well.

> I'm always very busy running round after everybody else. I usually go down to talk to Lucy for a while, keep her company and then I go to a friend of mine down Little London, two or three times a week and then the rest of the time's my own ... I'd rather go and help somebody else, it's a lot better. Oh yes, if anybody needs any help, I would never say no if I could help them.

Some neighbours took on significant responsibilities for support, often incrementally. Two helped neighbours with bathing and a number were doing the cleaning on a regular basis.

Mrs Jones: 'Tis beginning to be difficult, to be honest, you realise you cannot do things any more. The lady next door comes in, she hoovers and does for me. We don't make it dirty. We are out tonight and she will come over, draw the curtains and put the lights on.

Q: So there is a very strong neighbourliness?

Mrs Jones: Especially between us two, but the others are all right too. On the other side, they've been here for a couple of years, very quiet, you rarely see them. We get a Christmas card from them, give you a wave.

Mr Spencer's neighbour, who also 'shopped for her friend round the corner', explained how she had gradually became more involved in his support.

I used to see them to talk to but I've never been one for pushing myself to go to people's homes but if I knew it was all right, I'd go and see them. I mean he was 93 and she was in her 80s. They used to go out but not like you are when you are younger and I used to think, 'Well it's a bit of company' and they used to like it. He does now. I used to do a little bit of shopping. I couldn't carry a whole load of shopping but she never asked me. She just used to ask me for odd things to bring them. When she died, I'd go over, make sure he's up on the morning, when he's somewhere to go.

I've been this morning. When I go to get my paper, I usually call and see if he wants anything from the shop because he forgets. I say 'Are you sure you've got sugar, are you sure you've got tea'. When I go into town, I pop in. You see that's another thing, I always have to go, 'Have you taken your tablets', because he forgets.

He'll ring and say, 'I'm just going in the bath. I'll give a ring when I get out, give me half an hour'. Then if he doesn't ring, I ring and if there is never any answer, I'd be straight over. But I think he should have someone calling.

It was clear that this neighbour, who dealt with medical emergencies and also routinely got Mr Spencer up in time for the day centre, was never involved in any care-planning discussions by professionals. The extent of her neighbourly support seemed to be invisible to the formal services.

Given the extent and nature of support provided by neighbours, we sought to identify boundaries around such help. Comments made at several of the focus groups highlighted real concerns about the extent of responsibility felt by neighbours for confused older people, focusing on the safety and security of the older person and their immediate neighbours.

Mrs Williams: I have an old lady living near me, she's 88 and her daughter-in-law and grandson come once a week on a Thursday to collect her pension or to bring groceries or take washing. She stays about two or three hours at the most. I go every day to give her tablets, she has a home help and she has two rails to go up and down steps which she can't manage really but she is very, very confused. She's always saying there's someone there and what they are doing to her. What can anybody do? We've had a doctor and he's given her tablets to see if it can help the confusion but it doesn't take it away.

Mrs Stoneham: Isn't there anything they can do?

Mrs Williams: No there isn't. She's on her own most of the time, apart from the home help calling or when I go at tea time but she wants someone that's going to go in more regular, maybe sit with her for a couple of hours ... But Maggie [Caring Together staff] has been to see her and she seems all right some times but she really worries me. She knocked me up the other night at 10.30 to say what had I done with all her tablets. Well I had to take them all away from her because they have started to bring them in another sheet which she had to take every day, but I can't leave her that sheet to take them because she won't know which to take even thought it does tell her on them ... They come once a week to see her but it's left to other people.

Mrs Green:	It's left to you, Freda isn't it?
Mrs Williams:	Maggie calls once a week.
Mrs Green:	Yes but you are on the doorstep.
Mrs Williams:	The home help can only do so much and she doesn't want them to clean for her, she doesn't want them to do that, she needs somebody there to sit with her to talk.
Mrs Green:	That's why she'd be better in a home.
Mrs Stoneham:	Yes she would.
Mrs Black:	She'd be better with other people like herself.
Mrs Williams:	She does her own cooking but she won't have a smoke alarm or anything, no she won't hear of it. I've tried to get her to have a smoke alarm. She has a big fire in the fireplace and she puts her nightie on there to warm.
Mrs Stoneham:	Oh my God! Who lives underneath?
Mrs Williams:	I do!

The perceived burden of responsibility in respect of people with dementia conveyed by Mrs Williams was shared by others in a similar relationship.

Paradoxically, despite the evidence of considerable neighbourly help and support, one recurrent theme throughout all the interviews was the decline in neighbourliness. Some residents from both Leeds and Hartlepool described a change to a less communal way of life, with neighbours out at work.

Mrs Redding: These days it is not as neighbourly as it used to be, you hardly see your neighbours, do you? You don't see hardly anybody these days as you used to do.

Q: Are they neighbourly in your block?

Mrs Redding: Yes they go to work, the lady next door takes her little boy to school, you see them going out to say hello to and that, but you never see them.

Q: So it doesn't work as a community where people pop in and do things?

Mrs Redding: No it isn't that kind. Not pop in for a cup of tea. Next door they are friendly people, at Christmas they invite us in for a drink or something like that. But that's it.

Particular difficulties were described in the high-rise tower blocks of Little London which had very transient populations and the Woodhouse areas which had high proportions of student residents.

I'm in the middle of a street and there used to be neighbours and now they are all students. You used to have all neighbours but now I've got three bits of paper with names on.

We sought to explore these perceptions further by examining the views and experiences of two nonagenarians. Both lived alone in the Woodhouse area: Mr Spencer, who had lost his wife in recent months and had periods of mild confusion, and Miss Marsh, who was visually impaired. With the exception of day centre attendance, neither of them had social care input from the statutory services but did receive substantial practical and personal help from friends and neighbours. Mr Spencer, for example, was receiving increasing practical and supportive help from one neighbour, another younger neighbour was employed to do his cleaning and laundry and the man next door tended his small garden. Despite the extensive help they received from friends and neighbours, both spoke of the loss of neighbourliness in today's society. Miss Marsh referred to the help she had when her mother was ill:

> Because you had neighbours in those days. You haven't today. They were all ready to help you.

Mr Spencer was asked if he could explain what he meant by lack of neighbourliness:

Mr Spencer: If you like, there were not one or two running things. You were all running it. You were all in one party. You see our family in Ranworth Terrace – all 15 houses – they were all neighbours. In those 15 houses, you could find, like my dad, he was a painter and he used to love gardening. He had a big green house, we used to keep rabbits. If they wanted to know anything about gardening or borrow any tools, go to Mr Dobbs. There was another chap – he used to mend boots. Mr Turner had a little hut in his garden – you used to take your boots down to him and he would stretch them – that is he used to put leather between the iron, so that they did not clang so much.

Q: So it is sharing?

Mr Spencer: Yes it is sharing. You don't find it today.

The loss they identified was that of an underpinning security of a close-knit community, of mutual support spanning the generations and involving everybody. This had been replaced by individual support offered by specific neighbours, greatly valued but seen also as more fragile and vulnerable to changing circumstances, as Miss Emsley explained:

My next door neighbour was an absolute angel but then her husband used to help her … Then he died and she stopped using the car. She was an absolute rock but now she can probably barely get her own shopping in. She's had a hip or a knee done I think. She can't get around much and she's on her own so I couldn't ask her to shop. So there's nobody really.

In general, however, the level and intensity of support provided by neighbours in Leeds and Hartlepool were notable. Much of it was provided by older people for older people, and was rooted in long-standing practices of neighbourly support. This may lead to questions about the sustainability of such support networks in future generations. However, there were also examples of help offered by younger new neighbours to the older people and, importantly, evidence of older people who had moved into the area recently being included in neighbourly support networks.

Formal neighbouring or volunteering

In addition to the support older people gave to their neighbours, many of those who were active were involved in a more formalised type of help giving as volunteers or members of self-help groups. RRN members, for example, had helped to set up and run a friendship group or were actively involved in the Widows Association. Others had organised social activities for a group of younger disabled people in their local community centre.

Caring Together had inserted itself into the local networks in such a way that, for some members, it was difficult to determine the boundaries of their activities. Mrs Redding, for example, following retirement as a home care assistant, had become a Caring Together friendly visitor. In this role she saw Mrs Coulter on a regular basis and provided social support, including help in building confidence after an acute medical condition by accompanying her to the post office to collect her pension. As a member of the local church she also visited Mrs Mitchell (also a member of Caring Together) and spoke of her visits to her aunt in the neighbouring area.

Mrs Redding: I am involved in both *[Caring Together and the church]*. I did a friendly visit this morning, on the way home I visited a lady and I'm hoping to go out again this afternoon to see another.

Q: So how many people are you keeping on eye on in this area?

Mrs Redding: For Caring Together, just one. Then we have a class leader in the church in this area, I've only got one that's not very well, the others you don't really have to visit them because you see them in church. I visit Kathleen because she hasn't been very well so I do visit her. If anybody is poorly and can't get to church we do try to visit them.

The friendly visiting scheme replicated and developed the type of informal support which had grown up in the locality. However, while much of the neighbourly support was offered by older people to older people, the Caring Together volunteers were drawn from all age groups. This provided another important dimension, namely the opportunity to develop relationships with younger people. Despite the neighbourhood problems discussed in Chapter 3 in relation to floating populations of younger people, there was little evidence of personal antagonism between older residents and students. Through the volunteer visiting scheme, people spoke both of friendships with students which carried on for years after they left the city and of relationships with younger people at work which maintained their interests in the wider world.

Summary

Social relationships with family, friends and neighbours were of enormous importance to the quality of life of older people. Social networks for older people are frequently characterised primarily as a source of support and practical help. However, while the structure and extent of individual networks differed, in general, parallel networks of family, friends and neighbours offered differing but overlapping opportunities for emotional, social, practical and personal support.

Friendships, offering shared experiences and memories, stimulation and fun, lit up people's stories of their day-to-day lives; their absence left a sense of emptiness and shadow. Whilst points of transition and life changes, such as retirement and bereavement, threatened some friendship networks, they equally posed the possibility of expanding networks through engagement in new interests and activities and regenerating relationships that had been important during earlier life stages but had been disrupted for different reasons.

Illness and increased disability had the potential to impact adversely on friendship networks. Crucial to their maintenance was whether people's social worlds came to them or their involvement in local groups offered them opportunities for sustaining relationships. The existence of local community-based groups that supported people's own efforts to remain socially connected both reinforced informal social networks and provided the spark to establish new links for those experiencing ill health and disability.

Within family networks, our study revealed a rich pattern of reciprocity and mutual exchange, with active older people playing a significant part as givers of help. As people became more limited by ill health or advanced old age, the flow of exchange shifted. Even so, acceptance of help from close family members was subject to complex negotiations and characterised by efforts to maintain balance.

With respect to both friends and family, including children, there was a sense of a boundary around the nature and level of support and help it was deemed appropriate to seek help about. Within both kinds of relationships, older people were anxious not to be a burden and to acknowledge that friends and family, including sons and daughters, had their own lives to lead. It was only in respect of 'intimate' relationships – not only a spouse, but also an intimate friend or 'soulmate' or lifelong companion – that there existed no such boundaries: support was unconditional, expressed in the phrase 'we're there for each other'.

In both localities, there was evidence of extensive neighbouring, involving men and women, an expression of, and contributing to, community spirit. This assumed manifest forms: a friendly face to say hello to, keeping an eye out for people, doing little errands, or helping out in a crisis. There were many examples as well of extensive, regular help provided by neighbours. Much of this involved support from older people to other older people, but it also crossed generations. Paradoxically, older people also remarked on what they saw as a decline in neighbourliness, whilst also providing accounts of the support they themselves received from neighbours. This was explained by the shift from the close-knit locality-based networks, spanning generations and embracing many people in a web of sharing and support, to individual support by specific neighbours, greatly valued but seen as more fragile.

As noted in Chapter 5, older people derived significant benefit from their community involvement, keeping active, having a purpose in life, developing new skills and making new friends. The extent of involvement of older people in volunteering was considerable. Thus, community centres, campaigning associations, tenants groups, luncheon clubs and self-help groups all relied heavily on older people. Civic engagement extended beyond those who were physically active. Many of those restricted to their own homes took an interest in issues of importance in their local area. The Neighbourhood Watch scheme in Woodhouse, for example, relied on an extensive telephone network involving people who were restricted to their homes.

In myriad ways, older people were an integral part of, and made an important contribution to, the social fabric of the study areas.

7 SUPPORT FROM SERVICES: EXPERIENCES AND ASPIRATIONS

In the preceding chapters we examined older people's experiences of ageing and the things that were important to them in sustaining well-being. Here, we focus on three distinct themes: first, older people's use of formal services in maintaining quality of life, and those features of service provision and delivery that posed difficulties for them; second, an alternative model of service delivery, specifically the neighbourhood network as epitomised by the approach of Caring Together; and third, older people's perceptions of the needs of others.

The information is drawn from the individual interviews and focus groups exploring the quality of life theme, and those additional focus groups that examined service preferences and priorities.

Experience of formal services

We have adopted a broad conception of service here, including not only social care and health, but also housing and income support.

'Having enough money'

Money was not a dominant theme in the interviews, although it was widely said that having enough money to be comfortable was important to a good quality of life. 'Health and wealth' was the tip-of-the-tongue response within some of the focus groups to the question 'what makes for a good life?' Those people who had more financial assets were more likely to raise the question of money. Women who had lived alone when they were of working age – those who were single, separated or widowed early – also referred to concerns about being able to manage financially when they left paid work. Miss Openshaw, who had retired early, found it hard in the beginning but 'since I had the state pension, I have managed quite successfully. I've never gone without food even when I was very hard up'. The people who felt badly off were those whose income or assets were just above income support levels.

The concept of 'having enough money', however, is highly subjective and must be placed in context. Many of those interviewed had worked all their lives, mostly in low-paid jobs; they also remembered financial hardships experienced in their childhood and the war years. Women bringing up children on their own spoke of lives of considerable toil to make ends meet: Mrs Evans, for example, had had three jobs while also bringing up her daughter by herself. Mrs Franklin remarked:

> When I was working on my own, I was a single mother. What I did with my two girls, I boarded them out and I paid for them to be somewhere they could be brought up properly. There were times when I used to go to work and all I had was a roll and a cup of tea for my lunch. But nobody knows … I'm going smiling.

There were frequent references to thrifty habits learned in earlier days and to the disparity between their values and attitudes to money and those of younger generations. Some older people noted that, in comparison with their younger days, they were generally better off now, in that material possessions and foreign holidays were within their reach. Even so, most did not have much in the way of material assets. As we saw earlier, home ownership was low within our sample as was car ownership, especially in Leeds.

The majority, however, spoke of having enough for their modest wants in their later years. This reflected the fact that they had some money over and above the basic state pension from varied sources, for example small savings, income support or disability benefits. At the same time, universal benefits such as free TV licences and subsidised travel were highly valued, although disparities between different localities were a source of anger and sense of injustice.

Several noted that, for the first time in their lives, they had a small amount of money to spare. They remarked on the fact that, after a lifetime of saving, they were able to treat themselves, for example by going on holiday. For those with grandchildren, being able to help them out financially was a common source of pleasure.

> For all the years, we've always been very careful about money because I was brought up in a generation when money was always tight. You never spent money unless you could afford it and then you always had to put some aside for a rainy day. Well it is raining now. My wife might as well buy things because we can afford it: we are not saving for the future. This is the future. But it is very difficult to get out of that way of thinking when all your life you have looked after money.

> All the time when the children were young we had no money and now when they are grown up, we have plenty coming in. We just spend it on our grandchildren.

Some people receiving benefits could not fully use them, in part because of lack of information about what was available; in part because they needed assistance to open up their options. Mr Fleming's experience illustrates the different kinds of knowledge required to make best use of what he got.

Mr Fleming: I've got all my money. I get £225 a week but money's nothing. I give my granddaughter so much money because it is no good to me. I have everything I want.

Q: But will that not pay for a personal assistant for you *[previously discussed in the interview]*?

Mr Fleming: I've never looked into anything like that you see, so I don't know. Nobody has explained to me how I could go about it. Even to take me into town, it would make a change for me ...

Q: What about holidays?

Mr Fleming: That's one thing I miss. I want to go away, but it is trying to find a place that caters for wheelchairs.

Attitudes to benefits varied: from ambivalence about their entitlement to forthright statements about the payback in old age for a lifetime of hard work. Mr and Mrs Tyson indicated the reasons for their ambivalence:

Mrs Tyson: This money we get, I feel guilty, don't I? I feel really guilty. All the years he worked, I've never had money like that.

Q: But instead of feeling guilty, couldn't you just enjoy it?

Mrs Tyson: I can now because as I've told you before we had no money to bury us with. Well I've put so much of it away I don't have to worry about that now. And our television broke down and we got a new one a fortnight since and I was able to pay for that.

Mr Tyson: But all our lives, we have never had any debt, we've never had anybody knock, knock, and knock. What we haven't been able to afford, we haven't got until we could afford it.

Mrs Mitchell considered she had earned what she got:

I'm not grumbling about anything I've got and what I've got I think I deserved. I've no compunction about taking the benefits because I think I've paid for it. I worked till I was 67, so all in all, I'm grateful for what I've got but I think to myself, I've paid for it. I'm not on the cadge.

Both the bureaucracy involved and the quality of information about what was available affected access to services. The systems in place to apply for benefits irked and mystified many people, especially where they involved liaison with more than one agency. Application forms were regarded as confusing and off-putting, 'a minefield of misleading information'.

When you get a form to fill in, you need to have six A levels and whatever and a barrister to fill it in for you.

Mrs Dalziel described the medical assessment for attendance allowance in graphic detail as a humiliating and upsetting episode.

Complexity of the system led to lack of clarity about entitlements and was off-putting for older people, so that good help and advice to take them through the maze were regarded as a necessity.

It is that sort of thing that gets people down. You get a form and you read it and think, 'what does this mean'. Sometimes I ring them up and they'll start waffling. I say, ' You don't know either do you?' But how do you fill these things in? And they say older people should claim this sort of money!

The small number of people who had occupational pensions and income from investments expressed worries about the stability of their own income and that of future generations of older people. Some of those who had limited private means resented their exclusion from support and services through means testing.

We don't get nothing. They don't give you nothing because they come and they ask you if it is your house and you say, 'Yes'. 'Well,' they say, 'We can't do it. If it was a corporation house, we could do it.' Even this morning when we went to the dentist, she asked me if we get anything. She said, 'You should get it'. But I said, 'No every time they come, they ask and then they say "no" because of my pension'. Just because I paid into a private pension, we are not entitled. So I don't worry myself.

Well, as I say, not everybody can claim. It's like me. I have a son at home. It is not my fault he won't go but I have only my bare pension at £78 odd. Now they turned round and told my son to keep me, I can't claim anything. So no way could I afford to go out and pay all that [day centre charge]. Well it isn't fair. I didn't know how much he drew and they gave me a form to fill in and you had to put down his wages and I didn't know. I get his board and that is it.

Liability for charges for social care services and housing led some of these older people to consider the value for money of what was on offer. There were examples of services such as home care being cancelled because they were not deemed to be good value.

Health

Whilst health was seen as fundamental to well-being, health services had a shadowy presence in the interviews, not featuring prominently in the day-to-day lives of most of those interviewed.

Older people emphasised their own efforts to manage their health and avoid 'bothering the doctor'. At the age of 93, Mr Spencer explained that if you contacted the surgery it often resulted in a hospital admission so he was very wary about this, preferring to rest in bed to see if he got better.

People's assumption of personal responsibility for their health shaped their expectations of what should be available to them when they required medical expertise. Prompt attention was expected.

Mrs Melville: You can't get a doctor till you are well again, can you? It takes about a week to get a doctor.

Mrs Mattocks: I try not to contact the doctor. It was nearly a week before I did. I got up to go and my legs wouldn't carry me. So I rang and he came and told me to go to bed, so I did.

Mrs Pelham: When I had an emergency, there is a clinic on Saturday morning. He was quite rude to me. He said, 'you know Saturday is an emergency'. And it was an emergency. I'd nowhere to turn.

Older people who were immobile or suffered from ill health were frustrated by fragmented or unco-ordinated primary care services. A number of people, all of whom attended day centres, mentioned that they or their housebound spouses had not received the flu vaccination because they could not get to the surgery. Miss Marsh was taken to the health clinic adjacent to her day centre for podiatry treatment: but she could not have her ears syringed by the nurse as she was not a patient at that practice. By way of contrast those local pharmacists who offered a delivery service were important health contacts for a number of older people. During two interviews, pharmacists or their assistants arrived to bring tablets. For Miss Goodman, the contact was like a visit from a friend or neighbour – she had a discussion with the assistant about her colleague's new baby, caught up on the news and sent her away with some freshly baked scones. The pharmacist himself delivered to Mr Spencer – there was careful discussion about what each tablet was for, when they should be taken and changes which the doctor had made to the regime.

A key feature of older people's conversation about primary care was their relationship with the GP. This was particularly marked among those who were more restricted and had more health contacts. A number of people developed a deep trust and respect for GPs who were seen as taking a special interest in them as individuals.

> It's funny when I ring for him – he's a busy doctor. The woman answers the phone and she always says, 'I don't know if it will be Dr B or not'. I think I do. It's always Dr B who comes unless he's on holiday.

A key point at which relationships were forged was when people were caring for a relative or friend, particularly in terminal care.

After my wife died, she used to come to see me, then she decided I was good enough to go down and see her but she said, 'Any time you can't manage, just phone up and I'll come and see you'. She is a marvellous doctor. She used to come in here and my wife would sit there and she used to kneel down and hold her hand and yet to see her, you would not think she would do anything like that. She came to the funeral.

Older people wanted health professionals to recognise their own contribution to their health. They wanted professionals to listen and understand what was important to them. Conversely, they were greatly irritated by patronising, ageist responses.

I know everybody has to wait their turn and the facilities are not adequate, but everybody has that problem. But if you come on your own without a grown son or relative, you feel as though you are expendable, just another person with arthritis and they decide what's enough for you. They grab something off the peg or they blame it on your age and they tell you what's good enough, whether it is acceptable to you or not. For instance, if you can go for your pension and get to the shops, that's enough for you. If you have any special interests, if you say, 'well I usually dance or something and I can't do it', it's like, 'what for, why do you need it'. They decide on you and me – not all of them, but you get a lot of that.

They treat you as if you are simple. People look at you and they talk at you and explain like you could not understand.

They get on your nerves, they talk to you like children. It does, it gets on my nerves. Well I've even said it to my daughter, 'I can think; I can read'. When I was at the Infirmary last time, the doctor – because my daughter goes with me – and he said, 'Well I'll write and tell your mother and that or shall I send the letter to you'. I said, 'Eh I'm here. I am the patient and I can hear you and I can see you and I can talk. Why do you have to tell her? She is not your patient'.

Some people expressed a real sense of powerlessness as service users. Miss Mills, who was deaf, had been referred by her GP for a new digital hearing aid four months earlier. 'They said I would hear in two to three weeks but now it's been over four months.' She was uncertain why this was the case but had not made enquiries about it.

I know there are cutbacks in the NHS but at my age I might have popped my clogs before I get one. If it could improve my hearing a bit, that would be good. I'm no good in company. It is very isolating.

Other people were reluctantly resigned, recognising that they were not getting the best possible treatment, but accepting it. Mr Brown spoke of how he felt at the onset of Parkinson's disease: 'I thought it was the body crying out for something'. He attended the surgery repeatedly until the condition was finally diagnosed. His view was that 'Our GP might have done more than what he is doing now, but I am still comfortable'.

A very few described being more assertive with their doctors and negotiating the treatment they required. Miss Emsley spoke of one of the older doctors at her surgery, who she had thought was 'all for the elderly'. He had told her that nothing could be done for her arthritis. Her view was that she was experiencing an acute problem which could be ameliorated by physiotherapy. After considerable argument she 'wangled an appointment with a physiotherapist' and then 'wangled about ten sessions out of her'. Having done the exercises she was given, the pain diminished. She felt angry and sad that when she tried to explain to the physiotherapist that her work had been effective, she kept 'drowning her out'. Mr Edmonds spoke of pressing his doctor to sort out his outpatient appointment, discussing the possibility of private treatment, which seemed to make the doctor more attentive.

Experience of acute hospitals – whether as patients themselves or emotionally involved with someone ill – was often marked by trauma and distress. Frequently it related to the death of a loved one, to people's own loss of physical ability or to tests to investigate worrying symptoms.

Across the whole health system, there was consistency about what older people valued: problems recognised promptly and dealt with speedily; empathetic, helpful and professional staff; good communication and information; high quality clinical treatment; and being respected as an individual. However, the interviews overall were characterised by accounts of patchy and inconsistent quality at both individual and service levels.

Social care

Home care

About one-third of those interviewed had some help from social services – mainly home care or day care. Those receiving home care were typical of such users generally, i.e. older (over 80), of limited mobility and living alone. However, there were other older, frail people in the sample who received no support from formal services.

What factors determined people's receipt of home care support? First, there was the availability of informal help from family or friends, to substitute for what they could not do themselves. For example, Mrs Healy's daughters visited twice a week to help with shopping, but as they did not live in the immediate locality, home care workers, calling twice daily, helped her to get up and dressed and prepared her meals.

Second, the attitude of the older person to accepting help from external sources, as well as the kind of help they deemed necessary, was also significant. A number of very old women defined their main need for assistance as help with cleaning but this was not provided by home care.

Third, there was the issue of how people came to the notice of services. Generally, formal contact with services occurred mostly at a point of crisis – hospital discharge, carer crisis or bereavement. In one focus group, it was suggested that a fall, followed by a hospital admission, was the surest and most direct route into formal services. Moreover, people whose needs were visible to those who were knowledgeable about the service system were more likely to be referred for help. This was not entirely related to need but could be affected by environmental factors. For example, in one of the sheltered housing complexes where the laundry room was difficult for people with mobility problems to access, several of the residents were put in touch with home care for help with their laundry.

People were very appreciative of the support they received. The fact that they could get help from outside the family helped to allay their concerns about being a burden.

> To be honest and truthful I don't feel so well but the home care people are very good to me. I have a cleaner comes once a fortnight and one every week that comes and does my shopping. I am on the warden's round which I get every day from one of them and they are all very kind and I appreciate it very much.

A highly valued aspect of home care was the relationship with care workers, which was frequently described in familial or good-neighbourly terms. Several lonely men in the sample, who had limited social support, were highly dependent on their care workers. They referred to them as 'like a mother to me' and spoke of consulting them about different hassles such as how to contact an optician, where to find suitable clothes, or where to get help on financial matters.

Other older people spoke of relationships with their care workers that resembled that with a close neighbour.

> My home care is a love. I've got her number and even if she is off duty, she will come.

Flexibility and responsiveness to informal negotiations about what help could be provided and how to access it were also valued. People believed that their care workers offered assistance over and above their defined duties. In part, workers themselves contributed to such a belief:

> I just have to ask [one of the girls] and they do it. I've no trouble in that respect. Even my personal things like the catalogue sometimes. I asked them to do it and they do it. They're not supposed to, they say 'we're not supposed to do that' but they usually do it.

In part, it was seen to reflect the relationship they had with the worker. Mrs Mitchell said that the home carers kept an eye on her and would pop in to help her to have a bath, 'if they had half an hour to spare'. Mr Perring praised the way care workers had not been 'clock-watching' when they provided terminal care for his wife.

Two factors seemed to enrich these relationships. First, several of the older women in receipt of services had worked as home carers or cleaners. Second, in the close-knit community of Woodhouse, some of the care workers were personally known to older people as the daughters of friends in the locality. Mrs

Myerscroft had a home care package arranged on discharge from hospital that she cancelled before it started. She said that she would have proceeded if she had been able to have her friend's daughter, a local woman, as her care worker.

> I thought if I could have had Val to come because I think she is a lovely person and I've always said if I have to have anybody it would be her.

There were delicate situations in some focus group discussions where concerns expressed by service users about the quality of the help they received from home care caused offence to others whose daughters worked in the service.

The relationships described with home care workers were significant both in their own terms and as mechanisms for enabling, or disabling, older people to feel in control of their daily lives. Service qualities – such as consistency, timeliness, thoroughness and efficiency – were seen as defining features of a good service. Their absence was seen to reflect primarily on the services or on 'those in the office' rather than on individual front-line workers.

Consistency of workers over time was central to those who were very frail and disabled. This was not only because it facilitated the development of personal relationships, but also because of the energy expended in getting new workers used to their ways. Miss Marsh and Mr King, both with visual impairments, stressed the importance of care staff understanding that everything had to go in a certain place so that they could find it.

> The people that come round to my house from social services sometimes I don't even know where they are from and don't know who is coming. These things I want to know because I don't want any strangers turning up at my house. I don't even know who they are and I like

to know these things. It seems to me that when social services make decisions, they don't include people like me who are blind or people in wheelchairs or whatever, because only we know the things we need, the things that make us comfortable with home help and that's the way they get to know the things that are needed.

It was evident when older people spoke about how they managed their lives that much thought, energy and ingenuity went into dealing with the impact of their physical difficulties on carrying out daily tasks. We noted earlier that people prioritised the tasks that they wanted to do and those things with which they required help. Yet, the scope and remit of provision limited how far people could influence services to do what they wanted. This was most evident in respect of help with cleaning. There existed a clear clash of culture and expectations between what older people wanted and what services deemed appropriate to offer. Where cleaning was provided as part of a package of care, it was the first element to be cancelled or reduced when the service was under pressure. At the same time, need for help with domestic tasks was increasingly being defined as outside the remit of home care provision.

Older people restricted to the home, especially older women, placed a high value on a tidy home. Since they either relied on people coming to them for social contact or they spent most of their time within four walls, the state of their home was a constant reminder of increasing frailty.

Mrs Jenkinson: I can't do my cleaning. I've got a balance problem, so I can't reach up or look down. I worked all my life. I was very active on a Friday, laid on my back on a Saturday. Life completely changed. I can't go out now unless someone takes me. So I'm in all the time in that grotty

> flat – we all are. Well, it's not a grotty flat. But you know, looking around – and you know you can't get up to do the curtains.

Mrs Overend: It is sitting there thinking about it. It gets on top of you.

Where people were offered cleaning, it was limited in scope and duration. Tasks like window cleaning or moving the furniture would not be done.

> Well I'd like to do my own thing, because people don't do what you want, do they? But I was used to lifting furniture and I can't do it and they don't do it. They don't go into the corners. I'd prefer to do my own but I have problems with walking.

> They don't clean like they used to do. This is one of the things I think is totally wrong. They are only allowed to do very small tasks that you can do yourself.

The recollections of Mrs Pelham, a former home care worker, from the vantage point of around fifteen years in retirement, served as a reminder that expectations and standards of different generations may always differ.

> Then again, I think attitudes of elderly people have had to change. I was on home care for all those years – I've told you before I loved it. I enjoyed the personalities, though some did annoy me. They used to say, 'I'm glad you've come – the other one didn't do the skirting board or she had no time to mop'. They wanted you to be on your hands and knees and we didn't do that. We would tidy up but they used to say, 'Well I used to do so and so' because a lot of them had been what we called scrub women in the old days. But they had to change their minds.

Whilst it was the case that older people evaluated the quality and standard of help they got against what they themselves used to do, the issues arising from the interviews were more fundamental. They went to the heart of what people considered to be those tasks that they could not do but which they could appropriately give over for others to do; and those activities that were central to their well-being and which they would not give up without a struggle.

Day care

Fifteen of those interviewed on a one-to-one basis attended a day centre. We also conducted two focus groups in day centres, involving an additional ten people. The perceived value of day care to individual older people was mixed.

The primary purpose of day care was social contact and something to do outside the home. The opportunity to meet people with common interests related to place, culture or experience of disability was seen as important. Where people attended centres near to where they lived, they met those they knew from the past and with whom they could share experiences. This could also be the basis for renewing friendships. In both

Meeting others at the day centre

Leeds and Hartlepool, members of focus groups spoke about the value of seeing people they had not met for years. A group of women in a Hartlepool day centre talked of the pleasure of being with those they had known when their daughters were at school together.

In describing the centre for the blind she attended, Miss Marsh's narrative was of the shared experience of visual impairment, unrelated to age. Here she learned new skills, such as how to use a bread-making machine, and was given help to access talking books and aids in the home. Mr King spoke of the huge benefit he derived from the camaraderie at a similar centre when he lost his sight.

At the same time, others spoke of the increasingly narrow range of activities on offer at centres and the fact that for men in particular, there was often little that catered to their interests. For some of those who were socially isolated as well, their need for companionship was not likely to be met in a day centre as they were 'not that type of person' to enjoy organised social activities.

The decision about continued attendance at day care involved balancing perceived costs and benefits. Mrs Coulter felt the benefits outweighed the work involved.

> To go, I get up at 6.00 a.m. and I have to sit here nearly 10–15 minutes and have a cup of tea before I dare start doing anything. When I come round to myself, I go in there and make my breakfast and then I come back and go in there and get washed and dressed. I have to have everything ready the night before so that I'm not looking for anything. Then I'm only just ready for 9.15 a.m. when the bus comes. I feel shattered when I get to the day centre. Then I come round when I've got there and I've settled down and I've enjoyed it and it was worth getting up at 6.00 a.m. if you are going to see somebody. I could sit here all day and not see a soul.

Others limited their attendance to a single day for fear of being bored. Mr Andrews commented:

> I'm quite happy going to the centre once a week. I can go every day if I want but I don't want to go every day because I might get fed up with it that way.

Housing with care or sheltered housing

For those who had moved into sheltered accommodation, the precipitating factors were perceived needs for security, safety and companionship. It was often about feeling alone and insecure following a bereavement. Declining health or mobility was also a factor and the move was to ensure they had access to more support. In many cases, their families had urged them to move for additional security, particularly following harassment or crime.

Many had been able to move within their own locality or town but others had lost touch with neighbours in the move. Housing complexes varied in the extent to which they facilitated people meeting each other and making new friends. Older people were interviewed from seven schemes in the two localities: two in Hartlepool and five in Leeds. In one, there was clear evidence of both regular communal socialising and neighbourly visiting; in others, some visiting took place on a neighbourly basis or there was an occasional meeting or social event.

> My neighbours are fantastic, very nice. The lady there and her sister across the way, we get on really well. We don't keep going into each other's house but she's there for me and she knows I'm there for her and her sister.

> In one respect I suppose everybody keeps to themselves but in a community like this, when we go down to the big lounge, we all have a good laugh.

A few schemes were characterised by the lack of such opportunities; and some of the loneliest people interviewed lived in sheltered accommodation.

> When you are at home, you don't see anybody, you don't talk to anybody from one day to another. I can't explain the feeling at all. There's nothing wrong, they are not nasty or anything like that, just that they are not sociable, nothing goes off there. This is it, it's the problem of old age.

There were concerns about the resistance of some residents to joining in activities. At one of the focus groups, people remarked on the impact on friends and neighbours of a move to a sheltered housing scheme.

> Caring Together used to do tea and toasted teacakes on a Tuesday morning. But residents did not want to come to that. This is what happens – they get sort of inward-looking and there is no one to jolly them along.

Most people regarded the attitude of the warden as the most significant factor in developing a sense of community; sometimes by their own efforts, sometimes with the help of a catalyst from a community worker or outside group. Residents at one of the Hartlepool schemes viewed their warden's efforts as key to making it 'a very, very friendly place'.

In another complex in the town, Mrs Jennings observed significant changes.

> If you talk to people they get interested. Until Lucy *[community development worker]* started to go up to the scheme, there was nothing there. Now they have these fish and chip suppers and they have people in. The new warden as well encourages outsiders ... The board is full and you feel that there is something always going on.

People's expectations about additional security were on the whole met and many felt that the move had been very good on that count, as was the daily call from the warden.

One group were very upset at a policy change in their complex whereby the warden was to be non-resident. They spoke of their feelings of isolation and insecurity as a result of this development.

> And we don't feel that it is right because we are all over 80 more or less and we felt that we should *[have a resident warden]*. You know you pay for sheltered accommodation and we feel that it isn't sheltered any more. There is a feeling of isolation.

The presence of a warden or caretaker who could help with small problems, such as light bulbs and other maintenance issues, was also highly prized.

Locality-based models of service: the example of Caring Together

As we have noted in earlier chapters, Caring Together assumes considerable significance in the lives of large numbers of older people in Woodhouse and Little London. As one of a number of neighbourhood networks established in Leeds some ten years earlier, the locality-based model was stimulated by the vision of those engaged in community development work who found a sympathetic ear among decision makers within the local authority and the social services department. Rooting itself in the local community and building alliances with existing groups and community activists, it has been able to mobilise the resources of older people in the locality, drawing upon and energising neighbourly networks and reservoirs of reciprocal support towards sustaining people's quality of life, even in the face of restrictions.

From the accounts of members across the age spectrum – those actively engaged in the day-to-day life of the group as volunteers, befrienders and decision makers, those for whom the social activities were a major source of enjoyment and fun as well as opportunities for renewing friendships, and those needing assistance to maintain social relationships and social activities – the value of the group was seen to reside in the fact that it offers:

- a sense of belonging and being able to help others

- opportunities to engage in social activities and develop new interests and skills

- accessible support and back-up in times of need

- practical help, guidance and advocacy.

The value of all aspects was enhanced by relationships with staff and by the organisation's roots in the local community.

Participation and reciprocal help

Reciprocal help and mutual support were said to be a defining feature of the group. The opportunity to be involved and to help others was a key motivator for many members of Caring Together. Among those active in the community, there were individuals who were engaged in many different facets of the work – befrienders, volunteers in the office, fundraisers, helpers at parties and members of the management committee as well as active participants in the social groups.

Members who were restricted to their homes were included in activities and enabled to help where possible. Mrs Healy, for example, had done much of the knitting for a large tapestry constructed by the group; others helped by providing goods for fundraising events. One impact of the research partnership was bringing to the fore and making explicit the significance of participation and reciprocal help for older people, thereby contributing to the development of this way of working during the course of the project. Such an understanding was of considerable importance, not only for existing members but in involving new people. There was a concern, shared by some active non-members and some people who had just joined, about the perceived stigma of belonging to an organisation for older people as signalling dependency.

> I personally am not ready yet because I've got other interests, I've still got a lot to do. But when that day comes I'll be ready.

> I have only just joined. You see when my friend was on about it, I was more or less independent. I've always been independent. I've never been one to hang onto somebody else.

The opportunity to be involved in helping others had meant that some who were reluctant to join organisations for 'old' people could assuage their concerns.

> Well I keep thinking we are not old even though we go to Caring Together, like elderly people, geriatrics and things like that. I think 'we are not elderly'.

Emphasis on reciprocity had another aspect: irritation with people who were considered to be 'takers'.

> That makes me cross. They'll take things but they won't put anything back.

Social activities, interests and skills

One distinguishing feature of neighbourhood-based community schemes like Caring Together is the diversity of people who are enabled to be involved. By providing transport and organising groups close to people's homes, they are able to engage members of very limited mobility in gentle exercise and small social groups.

> Since Caring Together came, things have been much better. We can meet friends, get out, we have transport to get us here which we could not do before. We get here and have a laugh and a chat. And as well as this group there are coffee mornings, sales, we have a Christmas party with great fun and lots of food. Even days out and trips.

Q: How is this different from before?

A1:   We didn't have people to talk to before.

A2:   We did in the old streets.

Issues of facilitation and dependency posed difficult questions in the context of people who tended to know each other, for example providing transport door to door for those seen as unable to get out and engaging volunteers to push people in wheelchairs on trips out. Many were grateful and clear that, without this support, they could not take part because of restricted mobility. Others were said to grumble and be jealous of this 'special attention'; there was gossip about some who were seen as not needing this help.

Taking part in a large group was difficult for some older people – those who were deaf commented on the problems they faced in this respect, while those who were becoming frailer found that it was too tiring. During the course of the research, Caring

Together developed alternative approaches: setting up small neighbourhood groups for people who had health or mobility problems and whose lives were increasingly restricted. One such group was comprised primarily of younger old people, who spoke about their surprise at the importance of the group in their lives. During the course of the research, we observed how members changed: they described how they grew in confidence, going out together to places they would not have dreamed of going less than a year before. They participated in a range of other groups relating to health promotion, stroke prevention and gentle exercise. They also went on trips to the theatre and visited gardens and stately homes.

The group also sought to expand outwards, drawing in older people who were more isolated. A coffee morning, organised by student volunteers in one of the tower blocks with a large older population, attracted active members of Caring Together, non-members and those who did not normally attend other social activities.

The organisation made considerable efforts to sustain forms of social engagement among those who were mostly restricted to their homes. There was

Men's group outing

a group of volunteer visitors who went to see people on a regular basis. It was clear that firm friendships had developed between some of the older people and their visitors; where the latter were students these carried on long after they had left the city. Other older people were involved in a reminiscence video celebrating life in the neighbourhood. The annual Christmas party was an opportunity to meet old friends and acquaintances, especially for those who went out infrequently, and was a highlight in their year. Mr Spencer (93), asked about what made life good, cited the party, which reactivated his sense of being alive.

> What makes a good life if you like, when they waken you up. Like when we were at the party, we forgot all us troubles, we joined the party.

But Caring Together also provided a range of opportunities for renewing friendships and providing companionship and stimulation through social and leisure activities for 'active' older people, responding creatively to members' suggestions. These included a choir, book exchange, swimming and a photography group. Enthusiasm for a 'sponsored stroll' in the local park had prompted the notion of a walking group, which was supported via a local health promotion initiative. Parts of the locality that had links to people's past but had been off limits because of concerns about safety became accessible in a group. Activities were also sought that would be specifically geared to men's interests.

For those actively involved in the running of Caring Together, there were two distinctive features of its way of working that enhanced their enjoyment. First, alongside their sense of responsibility was the sheer pleasure and fun to be had in doing things that were challenging and new, which they would not have conceived of doing on their own. Second, there was the sense of freedom of being part of something without having to assume the day-to-day responsibility. For Mrs Melville, having paid staff meant that as she and her peers got older, they could positively choose where to focus their energy – being engaged but not having to be fully responsible as she had had to be in her time as a leading community activist.

> We did not have these people like Caring Together *[staff]* who have the job to look after people because when we were doing things, ours was solely voluntary, the work we did for people in this area, after we had been at work all day … So this is why Caring Together makes a difference. You are free to do your own thing.

The downside was the sustainability of the group in the context of short-term and non-recurrent funding.

> Well, there is a lovely community spirit with the elderly but what will happen when these elderly people go – when we die? Who's going to build that community spirit? … The people that I was involved with *[in community groups]* were people from Woodhouse and we looked after Woodhouse people. What will happen later on, I don't know … as *[people]* now haven't lived in the area all their lives *[like us]*. They come from all different areas … Caring Together has pulled the community together. But it depends on how long Caring Together is financed. You see, we weren't financed for anything. We had to go round and collect the money ourselves. But it was for us too.

Accessible support

The importance of accessible support was cited across the range of older people, including the most active. In particular, those whose family was not in the immediate neighbourhood spoke about the reassurance of knowing that Caring Together was there if they needed help.

We always know if we do have any problems, we can ring staff up.

It's a great comfort and support.

Examples ranged from help when the smoke alarm battery malfunctioned, or help with preparing sandwiches when the home care did not turn up, to assistance on premature discharge from hospital. An important facet was not only the proximity and availability of the staff but the fact that the service was not bounded. While there was no expectation that staff would do everything, they were seen as people who might know who would help, giving them a trusted conduit into services.

Being part of the local community and on the grapevine was an important asset, though at the same time, working in a small neighbourhood required considerable tact and discretion. Trust in the confidentiality of staff had to be earned and even with very high levels of trust and respect for workers, there were those who did not wish anyone to know their business.

The quality of relationship which many members had with staff was commonly described in familial terms. The recent wedding of the volunteer co-ordinator had generated interest and excitement comparable to the wedding of a favourite niece or cousin. The quality of relationships depended not only upon the abilities of workers but upon a measure of continuity over time.

Practical help and advocacy

Many of the Caring Together members had benefited directly from practical help accessed through the organisation. The presence in the locality of a community organisation with so many members was a useful 'way in' for a number of statutory organisations. Thus, members benefited from a number of free 'services': spy-holes and security locks fitted by the police as anti-crime measures, the fitting of smoke alarms by the fire service, donations of long-life bulbs from the electricity board. In addition, help provided by the handyman, the volunteer gardener and the decorator was much in demand, although not all needs could be met. In respect of repair work to homes which was a source of some concern to householders, being guided by staff towards home maintenance organisations was seen as very helpful. Workers also were seen as playing a significant role in helping people to access benefits. Mr Winston could hardly express the extent of his gratitude for help around practical support in obtaining housing improvements.

> Yes whatsoever we can do we are satisfied and we are contented. Since we got close to Kate, we get a bit of something done for us – see what she has done for us there *[new heater]*. We get in touch with her and she gets this *[decorating]* so what more do you want. Yes she is mother to us, sister, friend. I can't tell you.

Caring Together staff also acted as advocates for individuals in contacts with services, for example in relation to housing difficulties or in accessing help from social and health agencies. In myriad ways then, as one part of the local networks of service resources which was more immediately accessible to older people, Caring Together assumed considerable significance in linking older people with advice, advocacy and assistance.

Service needs and priorities: unmet need

Above we have examined the experiences of service provision which were valued or seen as unhelpful by older people. These were described by individual older people in the one-to-one interviews but were confirmed and extended by others in a series of focus groups to explore service priorities and preferences which were organised in the final stages of the project fieldwork. Here we present further key themes emerging during those groups, which explored more general concerns about unmet need amongst older people.

In the one-to-one interviews, older people generally found it difficult to suggest ways of improving their quality of life and rarely framed this in service terms. They would talk rather of being able to get out to the shops or to see their friends. By looking at things on behalf of other older people, the focus groups elicited considerable concerns about unmet need in general.

Needs of 'other' people

Narratives in the focus groups were peopled by a cast of 'other' older people who were seen as needing help because they were isolated, lonely, awkward, miserable, depressed, or struggling. Three aspects of social isolation were of concern: first, that people were lonely and unhappy; second, that they were more vulnerable because of their isolation; and third, that they were less able to access services which might be of help to them.

As people talked about the lives of others whom they knew, there was a strong conviction that loneliness and isolation had serious adverse consequences and led directly to them becoming more frail, depressed or confused.

> My father was called Joe, he was just like this. He was so lonely. He just used to sit around in his house all day. I think he died of loneliness. I used to say to him, 'Dad, why not go to the centre'. But he said 'I'm not going with all these old women'. He got very lonely, not looking after himself properly. He just used to lie in front of the fire, sort of waiting to die. He would have loved a friend to call.

They have no hobbies, no nothing. They just sit and watch television. They can't be bothered to do anything. And this is why a lot of this happens.

If our friend had had a little more kindness where she was, I think she would still have been in that flat and independent. But nobody was prepared to do that, all you got was that is not what we are paid for.

Some of the commentary on this theme was negative – older people were frustrated by what they saw as the curmudgeonly or defeatist behaviour of others. Some acquaintances were described as 'loners' who rejected neighbourly attention.

There was a man like this on our landing, just across. His place was a real tip. We tried to invite him to things, like at Christmas when we had a drinks party. Everybody came except him. He was invited but he seemed to want to be alone. We kept an eye on him and one weekend his newspaper was sticking out of the door. This Friday, my daughter said she would knock to see if he was OK. He came to the door and he was very nasty about being disturbed. Next time I saw him, I apologised that my daughter had bothered him.

My brother-in-law – he comes to me one day a week. I pay his milk, I pay his papers. He wouldn't join anything like this. I've asked him to. He's terrible. He can't see. But he will not join, because he has his own house and he's single, he has never been married and nobody is going to know his affairs. So what can you do about anybody like that?

Others were seen as perverse in choices they made, rejecting, for example, opportunities to socialise at a day centre or join a group despite being lonely and having few activities.

Oh they say, 'I wouldn't go there, I wouldn't do this'. Well I say, 'stop on your own then all day, if you are so high up that you don't want to come'. I mean there are all sorts going off. I mean you get a bit bored sometimes but just go along.

However, as the conversations progressed, the focus group participants offered their own explanations about why some people found it difficult to engage. Notions of pride, independence and privacy were suggested.

I think it is when they start probing into all their business and how much money they have and things like that that put a lot of people off.

People get along and they get to a certain stage in life, they just want to go on in their own sweet way. They don't want any outsider coming in to tell them to do this, they don't want anybody telling them you should do this, you should have a bath. Just leave them if they want to be left alone. If they need help, their family can come up and see to their health. They've got their pride.

People are frightened of getting old. Well you see, I've never been until this year because I've always been mobile and it has taken me all these years to come round and it has been a great help going to a day centre and coming here to this group.

Many of those in the focus groups were themselves restricted by ill health and immobility and spoke from personal experience about the problems of social isolation. Issues which had been evident in the one-to-one interviews, such as coping with sudden changes in lifestyle and the loss of social contacts, were openly discussed.

You see I'm ill and I get lonely. The flat seems to be closing in. I was the life and soul of the party. I worked down there all hours – 60 hours a week as the caretaker. I knew everyone, had loads of people to chat to.

Oh yes, Caring Together has been a godsend. We all look forward to coming here, getting out. Otherwise we'd be stuck in a grotty old flat.

I have stayed in bed to pass the time – it sounds daft doesn't it.

Some old people won't go though – even when you tell them.

I would never have thought, if you had asked me, that I would be looking forward to this, sitting for an hour or so with a group of old crones. *[Laughter]* But I do, it is really important to us, a lifeline.

Those taking part in the groups were convinced of their value in offering fun and enjoyment and saw these as the solution for other people's isolation. There were particular concerns expressed about how to find appropriate social venues for men, who did not often join social groups, although they were seen as lonely and in need of company. Amongst other suggestions offered, a dating agency provoked much hilarity but led people to reflect on the lives of friends whose later life had been transformed by new relationships.

It's surprising what it does for you.

It's company in other words.

People were preoccupied about the vulnerability of those who are isolated. A key aspect for some who lived alone, which emerged in both the interviews and focus groups, was fear of being unable to get help in a crisis. In part, the reality of people's experience confirmed these fears – two of those interviewed had fallen and lain for prolonged periods on the floor unable to attract help. At its strongest, there was fear of dying and not being found.

> There are a lot of old people that live in the flats that don't see anybody except to pop in to see if they are living. I mean there are a lot of people that die in those flats and you don't know. Where I am you could be dead and they wouldn't know.

For some, a regular call from neighbourhood wardens was seen as the way in which older people's security was best addressed, although such a service was only patchily available and even where it did exist, it could not offer the kind of availability that would ensure that those who fell would not be left.

There was a special level of concern for the vulnerability of those older people who were seen as unable to look after themselves safely. For people who may be confused or withdrawn, like Joe, one person proposed the notion of an advocate who could provide support on a one-to-one basis, while others felt that he needed regular support and monitoring from home care services.

> It seems to me he needs an intermediary of some kind – a sort of guardian angel, you might say, who can perhaps arrange if his bedroom is a mess or his kitchen needs a good clean for someone to do those things for him. The thing is he has been prey to con men several times but if he could say 'Oh I'll just get my neighbour in or will you ring this number please'. It is having someone who will come in and not letting anybody over the door unless your angel sees them.

The discussions extended also to recognition of the risks to neighbours from the actions of confused elders and frequently concluded that older people who were severely confused or demented needed to be looked after in a care home, where they would be safer.

> It reminds me of many years ago there was an old lady who lived alone and her neighbours were worried she would quite literally blow the place up because she would leave the gas rings on and she would not have anybody come in. She did actually blow the kitchen wall out but it could have gone the other way. How do you balance independence against necessity and other people's lives as well? I mean the old person might be independent but maybe their neighbours also have rights. I don't want infestation coming through the walls so where is the line drawn?

An important area of concern to older people in the focus groups was that isolated people would be less likely to know about services which could offer them help. The local grapevine – informal chat with friends – was said to be a good source of information. This was the way most people identified their own access to community groups: where local services had provided help for an individual, that person had told his or her friends, thus leading to new members. This was apparent, for example, in the African-Caribbean community of Little London, where a few initial members had spread the word about Caring Together to others.

Mr Manning explained how his wife tried to guide acquaintances towards helping services:

> Well with Marjorie in particular, we meet elderly people around the shops and if they are not getting along too well, then she says, 'Have you been to the doctor, have you seen this and that'. You can help that way but that is

only a handful of people you see around. In small cases like that they can be helped, but otherwise they are behind locked doors.

However, it was recognised that those who had few social contacts, and particularly those who were restricted to their homes, might not be in touch with others to benefit from this local information. Furthermore, older people struggled with the complexity of the problems about how services might address the needs of those who were reluctant to accept help.

They spoke of their own relatives and neighbours who they felt would benefit from some help but who resisted any incursions into their privacy. One man, who had difficulty in walking, went half a mile up the hill to the post office rather than collect his money in the local shop where people would know him. Mrs Daltry, who had a long history of working for the local community, still had people who turned to her, rather than to local services, because she was perceived as a neighbour and not an official.

> I have one or two ladies that ring me in a panic if they get a form. I know if I rang Kate she would do it but they want me to do it and I visit them and take the forms down with the pension books and bank books and nobody else must – it is this feeling of knowing me really. And that I'm here, they've known me so long. However informal the officialdom, it's authority. Even the forms themselves scare them to death because it is from the authorities. And I just go, 'Go on give us it here. We'll sort it'.

Concerns that some people still fell through the net and were not being reached permeated a number of the focus groups. There was a real appreciation of the problems facing people 'outside the system' in accessing support and services. Similarly, problems of disseminating information to people were discussed – using local newspapers, radio and flyers and still apparently not reaching everyone.

Older people, particularly those who were active, thought that there should be more comprehensive coverage of the older population by formal services:

> The council should have a list of everybody in the town over a certain age and everybody should have a visitor at least once. They might turn round and say they did not want help, but there might be the odd person you pick up that needs somebody, that has no family or nobody to talk to.

> If a social worker or somebody went and talked to them or explained things to them, it might help.

What was of interest here was that when they talked of 'old people' in this context, they were not generally referring to themselves but to those whom they regarded as 'needing help'. Notable also was that although there was a real concern about those 'lost', the proposed solution in terms of surveillance and 'keeping an eye' out for people was seen to apply to those who were 'old' and 'vulnerable', i.e. people who needed looking after, people not like themselves.

At a more general level, in respect of people like themselves, what was frequently raised in both focus groups and individual interviews were concerns about security and safety at a community level. Fear of going out at night in particular meant that many dreaded the long winter evenings. Opportunities to go out as a group at night were valued by active older people who lived alone.

Many were delighted by the provision of security locks and lights for their houses, which made them feel safe. For those in blocks of flats in the inner city, there was considerable frustration at the lack of effectiveness of security measures taken to deal with crime, harassment and vandalism.

> If you have an outside intercom, it needs to be high up, so no one can touch it because in certain places they have set fire to the front of it so that you can't see. Even the spy-holes in the flats, they have burned them from the outside so no one can see through.

> When I went in the other day, there were two young fellows trying to get in and I just pulled the door. They pressed 49 and our flats only go up to 45. So I just whipped in and went into Lily's and said 'See if you can see them on the camera'. And somebody was letting them in. They were only young, so you see there is always somebody silly enough if they say, 'I've left my keys or I've come to see my nana'.

Services such as a concierge system for flats and, more generally, on-the-ground policing and rapid responses to 999 calls were advocated in this context, while the determined efforts of community wardens in Hartlepool were praised.

One aspect of this area of discussion was concern for local youth. Many of the problems alluded to above were laid at the door of young people. There was at the same time, in both Leeds and Hartlepool, regret about the widespread distrust felt of the young and a desire to see more done for young people.

> It is a shame that we class all the youngsters the same. You see two or three walking towards you, your bag is like that [clutched towards her]. You think, 'are they going to make a move towards me'. You are walking along scared and they will probably move out of the way so that you don't have to walk round them. Decent kids and it is such a shame.

> There's nowhere for the children to go really is there. Not like when we were young. You could go to the swimming baths at the end of the street or you could go to the cinema. There were plenty of youth clubs. I don't think there are any now.

These concerns reflected an appreciation of the nature of an inclusive community which had been articulated in the one-to-one interviews.

Worries about not knowing where they could get help were linked to perceptions of unmet needs. People were described as needing a bit of help, and being unable to keep up their homes as they used to. Some were aware that neighbours' flats were in a mess. In the previous chapter we explored the high value which those restricted to their homes placed on cleaning services and the difficulties they had in obtaining such help. In this respect having sufficient money was seen to open all doors.

> How can you pay that out of a pension?

> That is just what I am trying to tell you, money speaks all languages. You have got to have somebody cheap. If Mrs So and So is £5 cheaper than Mrs So and So, you get her, whether it is clean or not. If you want owt, you've got to pay for it to be done.

> If you want your feet doing, if you want to go through the NHS, then you have got to wait. But if you ring the chiropodist, they will come and do your feet tomorrow. But you are paying the bill.

Help with routine maintenance and 'odd jobs', such as decorating, gardening, fixing handrails in bathrooms, or replacing smoke alarm batteries, was part of this debate on 'unmet need' in a number of the focus groups. Indeed, one of the motivating factors for setting up the RRN was the idea of a mutual skills exchange. People spoke of the register they had compiled of skills they could share with each other. Generally, these did not tend to address the issues people were worried about but reflected their own interests and skills: aromatherapy, cake making and icing etc.

The term 'low-level services', which is usually applied to such tasks, has been avoided with difficulty in the previous discussion. The high value placed by older people on help with small daily tasks and their impact on quality of life means that a new way of labelling such services is required, if we are to accurately reflect older people's preferences.

Summary

The descriptions of service experiences above have indicated that services offer valued practical resources to help people to maintain their quality of life. In considering older people's priorities for service provision, the following themes emerge.

First, formal service support is only a part, in many cases a small part, of the resources used by older people to meet this range of needs. Even the frailest older people invested significant time and energy in taking responsibility for and looking after themselves, while a substantial input of help from family, friends and neighbours on a day-to-day basis was evident for many. Older people were frustrated when formal services appeared neither to understand their contribution to, or value their expertise about, meeting their own needs. There was also frustration and anger when, after trying hard to rely on their own resources, they asked for help and were treated as if they were making unreasonable demands.

Second, when older people talked about the local neighbourhood and wider community, in terms of both the physical and social environments, they held values formed in earlier times. On an individual level, this could mean a dissonance between what they regarded as a good service (in respect of cleaning their home, for example) and what the services deemed to be a priority. At a collective level, they expressed frustration when other local people and even the local authority appeared not to hold notions of care for the environment as a high priority and were unresponsive to their concerns in this regard. Valuing and drawing upon the collective experience of older people in their localities offers a significant resource for the whole community and an essential component of neighbourhood regeneration.

Third, the importance to older people of being treated with dignity and respect – not stereotyped and not ignored as old and therefore incompetent – emerged loud and clear in people's comments about services. This applied in general terms with pleas against ageism, but also in respect of their individual experiences. Very high value was placed on interactions with staff in all organisations where a personal relationship was developed. The model which attracted older people was that of a 'neighbourly' approach by staff at grass-roots level – friendly, responsive and flexible.

On a day-to-day basis, the hurdles to be overcome in accessing services caused difficulties for older people. At the same time, what also emerged was the need for service responses that are in tune with their key values. Thus, what was seen as significant about Caring Together was the flexible and unbounded nature of its response, its base in mutuality and reciprocity, and its attempts to engage older people on their own terms in decision making and then acting on their ideas. Such schemes in local neighbourhoods could both be part of a network of other community groups and offer a valued link between older people and a range of formal, statutory services.

As older people reflected generally on others in their communities, their concerns focused on finding ways of reaching out to those who were socially isolated and whose needs were seen as unmet. At one level, their priorities for themselves and for others were similar: opportunities for social engagement; an accessible point of contact for advice, support, help and advocacy, both in crisis and ongoing; measures to address safety and security on a community-wide basis; and help with the kinds of tasks which posed increasing difficulties. What was regarded as vital was substituting for things which they could not do, whilst enabling them to continue to do what they could do.

At another level, what was also expressed was a certain dissonance between priorities for themselves and priorities for 'others' in the sense of those who were 'old' and 'vulnerable' and in their eyes needing to be 'looked after'. It is relevant, therefore, in developing understanding of need and service preferences that consideration be given to diverse voices and the context and social situation of those who are articulating such preferences and priorities.

8   Conclusions

Through the experiences and voices of older people, we have sought to provide a picture of what it is like to grow old in two different urban environments: inner-city Leeds and the town of Hartlepool, in North East England. Two broad questions guided the study: what makes for a 'good' life in old age; and what kinds of services and support could sustain and optimise well-being as people age.

In this final chapter, we draw together the connections between ageing, the features of the places and neighbourhoods where older people live, and the material and social conditions that both impact on their lives and affect their well-being in old age. This then provides the backdrop to a consideration of service preferences and priorities.

There are facets of ageing that are common to us all and the accounts of older people reveal a rich and nuanced picture of how people make sense of, and adapt to, the physical, social, interpersonal and psychological changes that are a part of the process. But the experience of ageing is also significantly shaped and influenced by the wider social context of people's lives, which was explored here through the prism of the localities where people lived.

A 'good' old age

For people in our study, ageing was simultaneously about opportunity and loss, change and adjustment. The meaning of these changes for older people and the strategies they employed to deal with them were influenced by a set of values that had been shaped by their life experiences and circumstances and the resources – psychological, social, cultural and economic – that they could draw upon.

Values

For most of the older people interviewed, their descriptions of growing up, working and bringing up families echoed the accounts of working-class life found in the community studies carried out in the aftermath of the Second World War (Sheldon, 1948; Townsend, 1957; Young and Wilmott, 1957). Whilst they struggled to survive on low wages and had few material possessions, their narratives were full of references to the close-knit, homogeneous communities in which they were brought up, and the strong ties of mutuality and friendship that linked extended family and neighbours. Themes of 'caring for' and 'caring about' dominated their descriptions of family and community life through their youth and into middle age. This was reflected in their accounts of 'neighbourliness' – both the mutual support that was offered in adversity and the routine reciprocal exchanges that were part of daily life. It was also revealed in their stories of the two-way flow of care and support across the generations between family members. For most women in the study, this culminated in 'caregiving': namely, the provision of practical support and care, often in their own homes, to frail parents and other relatives.

Now their own ageing was experienced in a very different social and material context: the enveloping framework of a welfare system that aims to provide a minimum level of security and safety for all; urban environments where poverty and deprivation sit in close proximity to economic prosperity and the trappings of wealth; the fragmentation and regeneration of neighbourhoods and communities and their cultural and ethnic heterogeneity; and the social and geographical mobility of children. But whilst these changes reflected some of the features of discontinuity between their past and present lives, the central and underpinning value they carried through into old age and which informed their conception of a 'good' old age was interdependence. The notion of interdependence held within it a number of key values that at first sight might appear to be in conflict. These were: the importance attached to being part of a community where people cared about, and looked out for, each other; a determination 'not to be a burden' on close family and, in this sense, to be 'independent'; and an emphasis on helping each other and maintaining reciprocity in relationships. Success in managing the changes that accompanied ageing, then, was in large part determined by the extent to which people were able to maintain interdependent lives: being able to view themselves as both givers and receivers of emotional, social and practical support.

Opportunity and loss, change and adjustment

For older people in our study, ageing was not simply about decline. It was not even about holding on or maintaining an even keel. It was about actively managing the transitions and changes that occurred in their lives, opening out opportunities and expanding horizons.

A key marker or point of transition to a different stage of life for most people in the study was retirement from paid work. This applied equally to men and women. Whilst the meaning of retirement depended on the context in which it occurred and the extent to which it took place at a time of one's choosing, leaving paid work for many was viewed as ushering in a new period in their lives, freed from the demands of paid work, domestic routines and family responsibilities.

As with any major life change, however, there were interwoven themes of loss and opportunity, especially at the point of transition: loss of income, routines and workmates, and more time and energy to spend on doing the things that offered pleasure, meaning and stimulation.

There was not a single lifestyle that defined a 'good' post-retirement phase. It could just as easily mean a slowing down to a gentle rhythm of daily life, 'rest and peace' from arduous physical labour, the pursuit of diverse social, leisure and learning activities, enjoying spending time with one's partner or the forging of new friendships. Positive adjustment, however, demanded that you 'worked' at retirement. At the same time, events or circumstances outside one's control – ill health, caring responsibilities or the death of a partner – could exacerbate the problems of adjustment.

Many women and some men also had to deal with the death of a partner during the early years post-retirement. Where people had established interests or friendship networks, these could provide the basis for adjustment and managing a new life. Whilst the loss of intimacy that ensued with the death of a partner, soulmate or close friend could not easily be compensated for, there were other opportunities that opened up, described particularly vividly by women. For example, developing new friendships, or participating in leisure and community activities that the freedom of being alone allowed, was described by women especially as a period of the 'flowering of old age'. For many of them as well, it was their involvement in our partner groups that extended their vision and scope for enjoyment, stimulation and a sense of belonging. For most men, on the other hand, it was the loss of intimacy and companionship that resulted from the death of a spouse that was uppermost.

Keeping well, maintaining health

Although generally people talked of health and functioning as major sources of well-being, a more nuanced picture was revealed through more in-depth exploration. For active older people, emphasis was on maintaining 'healthy' minds and bodies. This reflected awareness that a feature of ageing was that good health could not be taken for granted, that the body was wearing out and that positive action was required to nourish body and mind. But physical ill health and disability were also a focus of anticipatory fear, primarily because of the separate and combined impact on people's ability to maintain valued social relationships and social activities.

But if sustaining physical health was important, maintaining mental health assumed equal if not more significance as people aged. Across the spectrum of old age, a central theme in people's stories was the need for stimulation and involvement – keeping their minds active – not only retaining an interest in the world and in people around them but being part of, and contributing to, a lively and interesting social life. The other side of the coin, however, was an intense fear of 'losing one's mind' through dementia, for example, seen as an even greater threat to well-being than the loss of physical health.

As people moved through old age, restrictions on functional abilities as a result of chronic illness and the depletion of vigour and energy through the 'weight of years' were responded to, typically with considerable resilience. Even among those who experienced considerable loss of health and mobility, their stories illustrated an ongoing struggle for equilibrium to maintain what was valued, despite the shifting of the goalposts: 'Things keep throwing me back; then I start to get climbing again'. Even so, there were some circumstances that challenged people's capacity for adaptation to the limit. When the change was sudden and/or catastrophic like a serious acute illness or onset of major disability following a stroke, it could result in a profound sense of discontinuity between past and present lives. This sense of discontinuity in turn could give rise to depression and despair, further exacerbating ill health and functional abilities. For those in advanced old age – those in their eighties and beyond – there tended to be an acceleration and accumulation of loss: of partners, friends and siblings through death, coupled with their own ill health and declining mobility. Well-being here was not only conceived of in terms of the 'here and now', but in the context of an appraisal of one's life as being 'well lived'.

Social relationships

Central to well-being in old age were people's links to others: not just family but friends, neighbours and the wider community. Helping others and doing things with them – whether just having a laugh, engaging in leisure or other pursuits or taking part in collective action to make things better – enhanced people's capacity and confidence to cope with their own difficulties.

Some relationships provided the link to people and places that offered a sense of continuity between their past and present lives; others were rooted in their expressed needs for intimacy, support and companionship and were based on reciprocity and mutuality of interests and experiences. But older people also sought to sustain pursuits and activities that were a source of pleasure and meaning. Just because people were immobile did not mean they gave up wanting fun and joy in their lives. They also tried to achieve some continuity between the things that gave them pleasure in the past and now. Thus, whilst the form of social relationships and social activities might change over the ageing process, their essence remained critical to well-being.

Although people's spatial worlds inevitably contracted as a result of ill health, disability and reduced energy and vigour, this did not necessarily mean that people's social worlds also contracted or that well-being was compromised. Key factors were whether people's social worlds came to them, or they were enabled to maintain interdependent and meaningful lives, participating in and contributing to social relationships and social activities.

Participation and engagement

In different ways, and reflecting their different objectives, both partner groups illustrate the fact that older people represent an enormous resource in building 'healthy' communities. Valuing and drawing upon the collective experience of older people in their localities offers a significant resource for the whole community and an essential component of neighbourhood regeneration. Thus, the RRN provides an important forum for older people to engage in social action towards making a better life for themselves and their peers. Caring Together plays a significant role in the everyday lives of many older people in its catchment locality.

Engaging older people in action to secure a 'better life' requires a range of opportunities for participation, myriad levels of engagement and support and assistance to draw out from the deep well of experience and abilities. Moreover, threats such as frailty, disability and bereavement will temporarily or permanently deplete people's capacity and momentum for involvement. The focus therefore has to be on developing strategies for involvement that are both inclusive and continuously evolving and renewing.

Neighbourhood and community

A central theme in the study was the significance of place in the lives of older people. In part, this reflected the length of time they had lived in particular neighbourhoods, their familiarity with its physical and social landscape and their sense of community, namely the ties of mutuality, caring and belonging between people who shared common spaces that brought them into frequent contact with each other. For many older people too, this sense of community translated into action – whether at the individual or collective level – towards making life better for others in their neighbourhood.

More than three-quarters of older people in the study had lived in the same locality for 20 years or more (including those who had come as immigrants), and a third of them had been born there. But if their lives were characterised by stability of residence, the world around them had changed dramatically.

For those older people in Woodhouse and Hartlepool who had lived most of their lives in the same place, significant life events and experiences were connected in memory with physical features of the landscape around them. Continuity of friends and acquaintances over time provided a link between the past and the present, reinforcing people's sense of belonging. Even among those who were not personally known to each other, being able to share memories of people and places they had in common contributed to a perception of being part of a community. Older people here expressed strongly held values of mutuality, 'looking out for each other' and neighbourliness that extended to those who were newcomers to the area.

For older people in Woodhouse, the strength of their attachment to the locality was maintained despite the changes that had occurred in the physical and social environment: a transitory population of students with little investment in the neighbourhood, a dearth of local shops and services, and high crime rates. Thus, although to the outsider it seemed to epitomise inner-city decline, it was nevertheless rich in social capital, those features of social organisation such as networks, norms and trust that facilitate co-ordination and co-operation for mutual benefit (Putnam, 1993). Within its clearly defined boundaries, there existed deep and interlocking community links that embraced churches, social clubs, tenants associations and community-based groups like Caring Together. Older people were central pillars, sustaining and reinforcing these linkages and providing the continuity between the past and the present. Thus, some of those active in community groups in previous periods of their life had, as they got older, become active in Caring Together, with the explicit purpose of helping to make life better for older people in the locality.

Older people in Little London tended not to have such long-standing residence in the neighbourhood. However, although they did not express the same sense of attachment, neighbourly relations – having a chat, doing errands, sharing information, helping out in a crisis – were a feature of life in the immediate street or close where people lived.

Locality assumed even more importance in the lives of older people whose spatial worlds contracted as a result of ill health, disability and reduced energy and vigour. Even so, people placed high value on 'getting out and about'. Getting to the shops, for example, was not just about having sufficient food; it was equally, if not more, about the routine encounters with friends and acquaintances in the street and at the bus stop that reinforced one's sense of being part of social life.

Locality was also the prism through which the interaction between ageing, physical and social environment and socio-economic circumstances was reflected. The physical terrain – hills, narrow and uneven footpaths – created obstacles in negotiating the environment; reliance on public transport meant that existing bus routes, for instance, circumscribed where people could go; fear and insecurity on the street shaped the structure of one's day – out during daylight hours and behind one's door with the fall of darkness; access to a car, or having enough money to afford a taxi, meant that one could get out and about despite problems with mobility. These varied features of locality interacted with each other in myriad, complex ways. For example, for those older people in inner-city Leeds who relied on public transport, where they could go and what they could do was constrained by the nature of the bus route in operation and the frequency and timing of the buses. Whilst the Access bus offered more flexibility to those who were less mobile, the fact that people were only entitled to one trip a week meant that they had to choose between competing valued activities.

Service preferences and priorities

Formal service provision

For older people in the study, securing a 'good' old age was primarily about maintaining an 'ordinary life': 'enough' money to live on and provide treats for themselves and those close to them; the wherewithal to continue doing things from which they derived pleasure and stimulation; opportunities for social relationships and social engagement; an accessible point of contact for advice, support, help and advocacy, both in crisis and ongoing; a comfortable, clean and safe environment in which to live; an accessible, secure and negotiable external environment; and help with the kinds of tasks which posed increasing difficulties. In this respect, needs and service preferences in old age were no different than at other stages in life in that they encompassed service solutions spanning the economic, social and environmental spheres, albeit in the context of the changes and transitions that accompanied the process of ageing.

For most of the older people in the study, change and adjustment as a result of ageing were managed through their own efforts and with the support of family, friends and neighbours. Whilst many of them also routinely came into contact with health services, this was peripheral to their own ongoing strategies towards maintaining their own well-being.

However, some people also required specific assistance from health and social care agencies that was viewed as central to their continued well-being. Some of them, moreover, had been able to access appropriate support at the point they needed it; they had also developed good relationships with staff providing help, which was underpinned by mutual trust, respect and concern. However, the overall impression from the study was that many older people struggled to find the assistance they required. From the experience of service use as well, there existed a considerable gap between the rhetoric of needs-led and user-centred health and social care provision and the reality, both in terms of the range and types of services available and the culture and practice of service delivery.

Flexible, informal and sensitive access

In their encounters with health and social care agencies, many older people were confronted with systems and services that typically were perceived to be insensitive and unresponsive to their individual needs. They were faced with layers of barriers at the point they identified a need for assistance. These included: lack of knowledge as to what might be available and how to access it; low expectations based on their awareness and experience of what was currently available; and powerlessness in finding their way through systems and processes for establishing eligibility. Many needing help came to the notice of services either in a crisis or as a result of a 'revelatory' event, for example the death of a carer spouse or an acute hospital admission when their own resources for dealing with difficulties were at their most vulnerable. Some of them were more fortunate in that they had access to informal and trusted routes into services and support, either through friends and neighbours who were knowledgeable about formal support systems or community-based individuals and agencies that could offer a helping hand to access appropriate assistance.

Supporting interdependence

As we have noted above, it was interdependence rather than independence to which older people in our study aspired. In the context of support to facilitate interdependence, this had a number of facets. First, formal help was not just to be resorted to in the absence of supportive family and friends: it might indeed be preferable in order not to be perceived as a 'burden' on them. Second, whilst people identified need for practical help, they also sought to sustain social engagement and valued social activities, even when they experienced restrictions on account of a disability. Thus, support and assistance in securing opportunities for meeting people need to take into account people's specific interests and preferences. At the same time, the nature and form of the support offered must be geared toward securing an 'ordinary' life over the ageing process.

A rethinking of the meaning of person-centred planning

Even the frailest older people invested significant time and energy in taking responsibility for and looking after themselves. They experienced considerable frustration, then, when formal services appeared neither to understand their contribution nor even to value their expertise about their own needs.

From people's own stories of managing day-to-day life, they sought to prioritise those things that were important to them and, where necessary, draw on assistance from different sources to compensate for the things they could not do or enable them to continue carrying on doing the things they valued. However, there was often a mismatch between what services provided and what people prioritised as a need. The thorny and disputatious problem of the responsibility of services to secure a 'clean' home was posed in this regard. What also emerged were different facets of the problem as perceived by older people in different circumstances. It was evident that many 'active' older people prioritised going 'out and about' above doing housework. At the same time, since they spent a lot of time in the company of friends outside the home, they were not overly preoccupied with its appearance. At the other end of the spectrum, for older people who were restricted to the home, their immediate environment was of considerable significance to them. Carrying out manageable household tasks, like dusting, was often also part of their routine in organising the day. What they could not do were the heavy jobs that required strength, flexibility and agility – for example, hoovering, bending down to clean cupboards or reaching up to clean windows. Moreover, the need for formal services to help with these tasks was not equally distributed: both ability to pay and capacity to access reliable and affordable support affected need.

Services appeared to adopt a minimalist conception of what was appropriate, focusing primarily on responding to the physical demands of ageing, as opposed to the psychological, emotional, social and cultural impacts of the ageing process. Thus, whilst older caregivers might access respite services to enable them have a break from caregiving tasks, those who wanted to maintain a social life together with the person they cared for found it considerably more difficult to achieve: assistance to get out together socially was not generally viewed as an important and eligible service need. For people who required a considerable amount of help to enable them to live in their own homes, whilst home care support could be provided, what was not necessarily addressed was their need to maintain continuity of social relationships.

Forging a partnership between older people, professionals and service providers, if it is to have any meaning, has to start from an understanding of what is important to older people towards building upon and supporting people's own capacities and resources in managing restrictions and difficulties in their lives. Similarly, the conception of 'person-centred planning' must be broadened and deepened to encompass an understanding of the person in terms of their whole life – past experiences, current relationships, values, aspirations and goals – towards sustaining or reorienting those things that are valued and substituting for those that can no longer be accomplished.

Acknowledging diverse voices

As older people reflected generally on others in their communities, their concerns focused on finding ways of reaching out to those who were socially isolated and whose needs were seen as unmet. At one level, their concerns for themselves and for others were similar:

- opportunities for social engagement

- an accessible point of contact for advice, support, help and advocacy, both in crisis and ongoing

- measures to address safety and security on a community-wide basis

- help with the kinds of task that posed increasing difficulties in older age.

At another level, however, what was also expressed was a certain dissonance between priorities for themselves and priorities for 'others', in the sense of those who were 'old' and 'vulnerable' and in their eyes needing to be 'looked after'. This was particularly marked in discussions about older people who had dementia. It is relevant, therefore, in developing understanding of need and service preferences, that consideration be given to diverse voices and the context and social situation of those who are articulating such preferences and priorities.

Locality-based models of service

The neighbourhood-based model adopted by Caring Together offers important lessons in the construction of service solutions with older people.

Rooted in the community, and underpinned by values of neighbourly support, reciprocity and the engagement of older people at every level, Caring Together offers opportunities for sociability and friendship, education, social and stimulating activities, mutual support, practical assistance, advice and advocacy across the spectrum of old age. Indeed, key features of the approach of value to older people are: first, ways are sought to enable everyone – whatever their capacity and ability – to contribute to its work; and second, emphasis is on creative solutions to sustain people's social relationships, even in the face of restriction.

It is notable that Caring Together, in the way it engages older people in making life better for themselves and others, draws upon the weight of social capital in the locality and at the same time reinforces and extends its currency both in Woodhouse and into Little London. Thus, the social and leisure-based activities and groups which involve active older people facilitate the renewal of friendships and acquaintanceships that have been disrupted over the years of family and work life; the involvement of older people in community and voluntary action, including 'befriending' of others in the locality, enables people to give something to the community; and the many small neighbourhood groups established either around some common interest (book club, carers group) or physical proximity facilitate those who are more restricted to maintain activities and relationships. Moreover, its links with other community groups, including the churches, means that it draws in elders from minority ethnic communities, at all levels. In a very real sense, then, the locality-based model offers the potential to connect the expressed values and preferences of older people within a network of community groups to effect change at local level to support a 'good' old age.

Finally, the model provides the bridge linking older people within localities to different formal statutory services by enabling people to access timely and appropriate support. But it also offers an exemplar of what can be achieved in terms of quality of life for older people through an approach and service model rooted in, and building upon, the values and capacities of older people themselves.

Summary

This study has reinforced the conception of the 'duality of ageing' – old age as a stage in the life course that both offers new experiences and opportunities and requires adjustments to manage the losses that accompany ageing. However, whilst adjustment and adaptation characterised ageing, the process was neither smooth nor linear, reflecting in part the considerable variation between people in the resources and capacities they could draw upon in managing the changes that accompanied ageing.

The meaning and experience of old age need to be viewed within the wider social and cultural context of people's entire lives. It was evident from the research that adjustment and adaptation to the challenges of ageing do not occur in a neutral environment. First, older people were continually confronted with, and reproached by, attitudes and behaviour that devalued ageing and which they had also internalised. Second, they carried into old age the baggage they had brought with them from previous life stages. Some people in the study, for example, had small social networks or difficult and troubled relationships over many years that meant they had little in the way of social and emotional support to draw upon in old age. Conversely, people who had experienced chronic illness and physical disability throughout their lives talked about being better able to come to terms with restrictions in old age. Third, features of social structure – income and material assets that had been built up over a lifetime and the nature of the physical and social environments in which people lived – also impacted on adaptation and well-being.

From the experiences of older people, we identified the different kinds of obstacles and challenges that compromised older people's ability to maintain an 'ordinary life' and which might require support to overcome. First, there were the 'big' events such as bereavement or acute, life-threatening illness that changed fundamentally the rhythm and pattern of daily life and might require psychological and emotional support to manage. Second, there was the loss or disruption of valued social relationships and social activities that could impact adversely on people's life quality and required action to substitute for what was lost. Third, there were the 'daily hassles' that were a frequent source of stress and frustration, as well as constant reminders of the wear and tear produced by chronic ill health, disability and the weight of years. Fourth, there were the obstacles and challenges posed for older people in going about their daily lives produced by the physical and social environments of the places in which they lived, for example crime, the detritus of urban decay and the nature of the physical terrain. Fifth, there was the enormous gap between the stereotype of old age as uniformly negative and older people's efforts to construct a meaningful and productive life over the whole of the age span.

The overwhelming conclusion emerging is that securing well-being in old age requires understanding and action at many different levels: individual, neighbourhood, community and society. At the individual level, services and support which sustain 'healthy' ageing are those which open up opportunities for self-expression and engagement in social relationships and activities; provide practical, social and emotional support in coming to terms with and managing life changes; and offer assistance in dealing with the 'daily hassles' that constrain people's lives. At the neighbourhood or community level, securing well-being requires the creation of environments that are safe, secure and easily negotiated, as well as the integration of older people into decision-making structures and systems to effect positive change. At the societal level, it is about action to reduce inequalities and changes in attitudes and values that are discriminatory and that devalue ageing.

At each of these levels, the capacities of older people represent an undervalued resource not only in securing a better life for themselves in old age, but in contributing to the building of sustainable neighbourhoods for everyone. Focusing on ageing as representing a constellation of 'problems' that require 'interventions' ignores older people's own resilience in the face of difficulties and their own capacity, with proper resources, for organising themselves and devising their own solutions – at the individual and collective level.

REFERENCES

Andrews, M. (1999) 'The seductiveness of agelessness', *Ageing and Society*, Vol. 19, pp. 301–18

Arber, S. and Cooper, H. (1999) 'Gender differences in health in later life: the new paradox?', *Social Science and Medicine*, Vol. 48, pp. 61–76

Baltes, P. and Baltes, M. (1990) *Successful Ageing: Perspectives from the Behavioural Sciences*. Cambridge: Cambridge University Press

Baltes, M. and Carstensen, L. (1996) 'The process of successful ageing', *Ageing and Society*, Vol. 16, No. 4, pp. 397–422

Burgess, R. (1984) *In the Field: An Introduction to Field Research*. London: Allen & Unwin

Clausen, J.A. (1995) 'Gender, contexts and turning points in adult lives', in P. Moen, G.H. Elder Jr and K. Luscher (eds), with H.E. Quick, *Examining Lives in Context: Perspectives on the Ecology of Human Development* (pp. 365–98, APA Science Volumes). Washington, DC: American Psychological Association

Godfrey, M. (2001) 'Prevention: developing a framework for conceptualising and evaluating outcomes of preventive services for older people', *Health and Social Care in the Community*, Vol. 9, No. 2, pp. 89–99

Lazarus, R. and DeLongis, A. (1983) 'Psychological stress and coping in aging', *Journal of American Psychology*, Vol. 38, pp. 245–54

Phillipson, C., Bernard, M., Phillips, J. and Ogg, J. (2001) *The Family and Community Life of Older People: Social Networks and Social Support in Three Urban Areas*. London: Routledge

Putnam, R. (1993) 'The prosperous community, social capital and public life', *The American Prospect*, Spring, pp. 35–42

Riley, M. (1998) 'A life course approach: autobiographical notes', in J.Z. Giele and G.H. Elder Jr (eds) *Methods of Life Course Research: Qualitative and Quantitative Approaches*. Thousand Oaks, Calif.: Sage Publications

Scharf, T., Phillipson, C. and Smith, A.E. (2002) *Growing Older in Socially Deprived Areas: Social Exclusion in Later Life*. London: Help the Aged

Sheldon, S.H. (1948) *The Social Medicine of Old Age.* Oxford: Oxford University Press

Townsend, P. (1957) *The Family Life of Older People.* London: Routledge & Kegan Paul

Young, M. and Wilmott, P. (1957) *Family and Kinship in East London.* London: Routledge & Kegan Paul

APPENDIX

Characteristics of older people interviewed

Table A1 Location

	Frequency	Per cent
Woodhouse	32	37
Little London	27	32
University	3	4
Rift House	6	7
Fens	3	4
Owton Manor	8	10
Other Hartlepool	5	6
Total	84	100

Table A2 Age

	Frequency	Per cent
60–64	7	8
65–74	22	26
75–84	36	43
85–94	15	18
95 plus	3	4
Under 60	1	1
Total	84	100

Table A3 Gender

	Frequency	Per cent
Male	23	28
Female	61	72
Total	84	100

Table A4 Marital status

	Frequency	Per cent
Single	14	17
Married	25	30
Widowed	40	47
Divorced	5	6
Total	84	100

Table A5 Ethnicity

	Frequency	Per cent
White British	71	85
European	1	1
Asian	2	2
Black African-Caribbean	9	11
Other	1	1
Total	84	100

Table A6 Time in area

	Frequency	Per cent
Up to 5 years	2	2
5–19 years	12	15
20–39 years	20	22
40–59 years	16	19
59–79	3	4
Since birth	25	30
Not known	6	8
Total	84	100

Table A7 Type of house

	Frequency	Per cent
Flat	25	30
House	38	45
Sheltered accommodation	19	23
Bungalow	2	2
Total	84	100

Table A8 Household composition

	Frequency	Per cent
Alone	56	67
With spouse	24	29
With adult children	2	2
With other family member	2	2
Total	84	100

Table A9 Housing tenure

	Frequency	Per cent
Rented	51	61
Owner-occupied	33	39
Total	84	100

Table A10 Members of partner groups

	Frequency	Per cent
Yes	67	79
No	17	21
Total	84	100

Table A11 Needing help with managing day to day

	Frequency	Per cent
Completely independent	40	47
Help from family and friends	22	26
Help from formal services only	7	8
Help from family and formal services	15	19
Total	84	100

Table A12 Source of access

	Out and about		Restricted		Restricted to home	
	Leeds	Hartlepool	Leeds	Hartlepool	Leeds	Hartlepool
Via partner group	23	16	12	–	10	–
Via personal contact of older people	3	–	1	–	1	–
Via other community association	2	–	–	–	–	–
Via social services home care or day centre	–	–	2	–	2	–
Via sheltered housing (local authority or independent sector)	3	1	3	3	–	2

Table A13 Profile of the 'out and about' (*n* = 48)

	Leeds	Hartlepool
Living situation		
Lives alone	22	8
Lives with spouse	8	8
Lives with other (father, son)	1	1
Gender		
Men	8	4
Women	23	13
Age range		
Under 75	13	9
75–84	17	8
85+	1	–
Marital status		
Single	6	1
Widowed	13	8
Married	9	8
Divorced	3	–
Type of housing		
Sheltered	5	1
Ordinary	26	16

Table A14 Profile of those restricted to the neighbourhood (*n* = 21)

	Leeds	Hartlepool
Living situation		
Lives alone	14	3
Lives with spouse	2	–
Lives with other (father, son)	2	–
Gender		
Men	5	–
Women	13	3
Age range		
Under 75	3	1
75–84	6	2
85+	9	–
Marital status		
Single	4	1
Widowed	11	2
Married	2 (couple)	–
Divorced	1	–
Type of housing		
Sheltered	6	3
Ordinary	12	–

Table A15 Profile of those restricted to the home (*n* = 15)

	Leeds	Hartlepool
Living situation		
Lives alone	7	2
Lives with spouse	6 (2 couples)	–
Gender		
Men	6	–
Women	7	2
Age range		
Under 75	4	–
75–84	2	1
85+	7	1
Marital status		
Single	2	–
Widowed	4	2
Married	6 (2 couples)	–
Divorced	1	–
Type of housing		
Sheltered	2	2
Ordinary	11	–